Beauty, Honor, and Tradition

THE LEGACY OF PLAINS INDIAN SHIRTS

"And some years ago, back in early forties, I remember when I was a young lad. At that time, [some] men folks, were, say, about eighty years old. They would [get together] and sit down with a cushion—sit [together] on a cushion— and start talking in the past. They would talk about the war. And I was young, say, not even more than twelve years old. I [would] lay on my belly and listen to what they said. But it's saddening that those things [were not recorded because there were] no recording systems, no tape recorders. But those were some of the very important things that they mentioned . . . ."

Donald Stewart (Apsaalooke)

Beauty, Honor, and Tradition

THE LEGACY OF PLAINS INDIAN SHIRTS

by Joseph D. Horse Capture and George P. Horse Capture

National Museum of the American Indian,
Smithsonian Institution

The Minneapolis Institute of Arts

Distributed by the University of Minnesota Press

This publication was co-produced by The Minneapolis Institute of Arts and the National Museum of the American Indian, Smithsonian Institution, in conjunction with the exhibition "Beauty, Honor, and Tradition: The Legacy of Plains Indian Shirts."

Edited by Jodie L. Ahern and Holly A. Stewart

Photography courtesy of
  the National Museum of the American Indian, Smithsonian Institution;
  all photographs © Smithsonian Institution

Designed by MartinRoss Design

Production coordinated by Donald Leurquin

The Minneapolis Institute of Arts
2400 Third Avenue South
Minneapolis, Minnesota 55404

The National Museum of the American Indian
Smithsonian Institution
Washington, D.C. 20560

Library of Congress Catalog Card Number: 00-136515

ISBN
HC: 0-8166-3946-9
PB: 0-8166-3947-7

Beauty, Honor, and Tradition:
The Legacy of Plains Indian Shirts

by Joseph D. Horse Capture and George P. Horse Capture

CONTENTS

ACKNOWLEDGMENTS

We were fortunate to be part of this project, which has involved many good people who believe, as we do, that Plains Indian shirts comprise an important subject we need to explore.

These shirts were made to honor their male wearers. They are also a credit to the Plains Indian women who executed their intricate craftsmanship; it takes years of experience to comprehend and excel in the arts of beading, quilling, and shirt construction. The relationship between the man, whose accomplishments warranted the creation of the shirt, and the woman, who delicately crafted the powerful garment, is reflected in the artistic genius and emotional resonance embodied in each shirt.

We especially wish to thank the tribal elders and artists of the Blackfeet Indian Reservation, Northern Cheyenne Indian Reservation, Crow Indian Reservation, and Pine Ridge Indian Reservation, who welcomed us into their communities and shared their knowledge with us. We would also like to recognize the young men of the Heart Butte basketball team for sharing their experiences and ensuring that the future of Indian people is in good hands.

We would like to take this opportunity to thank those who have assisted us in our efforts to produce this catalogue to accompany the exhibition "Beauty, Honor, and Tradition: The Legacy of Plains Indian Shirts." This book would not have been published if not for the support of W. Richard West, Director, National Museum of the American Indian, Smithsonian Institution, and Evan M. Maurer, Director and President, The Minneapolis Institute of Arts and Curator of its Department of Africa, Oceania, and the Americas. Their encouragement—both personal and professional—made this catalogue possible.

At The Minneapolis Institute of Arts, we are grateful for the support of Molly Hennen, Administrative Assistant for the Department of Africa, Oceania, and the Americas, for her tireless assistance in the research of the shirts and the collectors. We would also like to thank Jodie Ahern, Managing Editor of Publications, for her efforts and dedication with the editing, and Don Leurquin, Director of Design and Editorial, for his leadership and professionalism with the coordination of this catalogue. We also recognize Laura DeBiaso, Administrator of Curatorial Affairs and Exhibitions, for her assistance with this project. We also thank Marty Skoro and Ross Rezac of MartinRoss Design for the elegant design of this book.

At the National Museum of the American Indian, we would like to thank Doug Evelyn, Deputy Director; Bruce Bernstein, Assistant Director for Cultural Resources; Jim Volkert, Assistant Director for Exhibitions; and Gerald McMaster, Deputy Assistant Director for Cultural Resources, for their assistance, encouragement, and support. We would also like to recognize Ann Silverman, Exhibition Project Manager, for her efforts in many aspects of the exhibition and catalogue.

Also thanks to Holly Stewart, Catalogue Co-editor; Amy Pickworth, Exhibition Editor; and Terence Winch, Head of Publications.

We are grateful to Katherine Fogden and the Photographic Department for their willing assistance in the many phases of this project. Additionally, many thanks are due to Kathy Suter and Dan Davis, Media Specialists, who made the Indian voice come alive in the exhibition.

Appreciation goes to Collections Manager Devorah Romanek, Marian Kaminitz, Head Conservator, Monika Harter, Conservation Fellow, and to their fellow conservators, and photo researcher Lou Stancari. Finally a sincere thanks to Myra Valdez-Lopez, who assisted with the research, and to all of the other staff who helped with the catalogue.

We appreciate the research assistance of James Keyser, U.S. Forest Service, and the trust of Dr. Alonzo Spang, Dull Knife Tribal College, for putting his wonderful war shirt into our care as a contemporary part of the exhibition.

We would also like to recognize our families. First and foremost we would like to thank Kay-Karol Horse Capture, for all of her editorial and typing assistance, above and beyond the call of duty. Also, we would like to thank Lisa Ranallo for her moral support while the catalogue was being written. Finally, we would like to thank six-year-old Singer Horse Capture for understanding that sometimes one has to dedicate oneself to a project in order to do a good job.

Many of these shirts were made when the Plains Indian people lived a lifestyle that we can only dream of. It is through their eyes that we try to see the future of Indian people. The makers of the beautiful shirts that adorn this catalogue were wonderful artists. This catalogue is dedicated to our ancestors, who will always be in our hearts and minds.

Joseph D. Horse Capture and George P. Horse Capture

Introduction

Since the early 1970s, The Minneapolis Institute of Arts has been actively involved in the presentation of Plains Indian arts and culture. This has been achieved through the permanent collection, three major exhibitions and publications, and a decades-long involvement with Native American communities in Minnesota and other western states. In light of this tradition we are especially proud of the efforts of our curator, Joseph D. Horse Capture, who has added an important new dimension to our scholarly programs and our efforts to bring a deeper understanding of Native American art and culture to our audiences here as well as in other sections of the country and abroad.

"Beauty, Honor and Tradition" is the first exhibition devoted to the rich and complex tradition of the warriors' shirts of the Plains. By bringing us the words and feelings of today's Plains people, the curators of this project, George P. Horse Capture and his son Joseph, have added an especially valuable dimension of cultural meaning to these shirts and the honorable traditions through which they developed. Our museum is pleased to have this opportunity of collaborating with the National Museum of the American Indian to bring this important project to a broad public audience.

Evan M. Maurer

Director and President of The Minneapolis Institute of Arts
Curator of the Department of Africa, Oceania, and the Americas

SECOND SKINS

A shirt is a kind of second skin, suggesting the presence of its wearer. This is especially true of Plains war shirts. The original owners of these shirts earned the right to wear them through acts of great bravery, deeds that are recounted in their decoration. Most of these men are no longer with us, but their spirits are present through these extraordinary, transcendent articles of clothing.

This book and the exhibition of the same name present some of the most evocative objects from the collections of the Smithsonian's National Museum of the American Indian. I first saw many of them and learned of their significance 45 years ago, when my father—a highly respected painter and teacher of studio art at Bacone College in Oklahoma—took my brother and me to visit what was then the Heye Foundation's Museum of the American Indian in New York.

As an artist, my father explained how the shirts were painted, and spoke of his deep appreciation for their aesthetic qualities. As a Cheyenne, he told us about the people who made and wore them, the times in which they lived, and the achievements and beliefs they re-created in their art. Indians place great importance on this kind of sharing of cultural knowledge and understanding across generations.

This book, too, represents the experience of a son and his father. Joseph Horse Capture (A'aninin [Gros Ventre]), curator at The Minneapolis Institute of Arts, and his father, NMAI curator George Horse Capture (A'aninin [Gros Ventre]), researched Plains shirts with elders and others at the Crow, Blackfeet, and Northern Cheyenne reservations in Montana, and Pine Ridge in South Dakota. A handful of the people they talked with remember listening as children to first-hand accounts of exploits in the Indian wars of the late nineteenth century, when the Plains' last free tribes were forced onto reservations. They and their younger colleagues have provided an illuminating wealth of insight and information about the history and symbolism of shirts made by their forebears. On behalf of the museum, I am very grateful to them for enriching our collections with their knowledge.

Equally important, people in every community the Horse Captures visited spoke of the importance of tradition in contemporary Native life. At the Crow Agency near Billings, Montana, tribal historian Joe Medicine Crow shared a remarkable story that conveys something enduring in Plains Indian cultures. During the Second World War—"by being in the wrong place at the wrong

9

time," as he puts it, with humility and humor—Medicine Crow, the grandson of a scout who rode with General Custer, completed the four acts of great bravery traditionally honored on the Plains. He touched an enemy in battle, captured a weapon, led a war party, and spirited horses away from an enemy camp. The last, he realizes, demands some explanation:

> During the last days of the war over there, there was a lot of confusion, you know, so a bunch of S.S. officers had got on their horses and taken off. They were heading back to Germany. And here's that sneaky old Crow Indian, now, following them and watching. So they camped for the night. I snuck in there and took all their damn horses, left them on foot. And my buddies surrounded them.
>
> These were beautiful horses—cavalry horses—tall horses, and beautiful. So I got on one, looked around there, and even sang a Crow victory song. All by myself, you know? Crows do that when they think they're all by themselves, they do things like that. So I sang a victory song.

In many ways, of course, the world has changed since then, and with it, Plains cultures. Yet Indian families and communities continue to honor perseverance in new theaters of accomplishment—in classrooms and on sports teams, for example. I am delighted to see shirts that celebrate these contemporary triumphs featured prominently here.

W. Richard West

(Southern Cheyenne and member of the Cheyenne and Arapaho Tribes of Oklahoma)
Director, National Museum of the American Indian, Smithsonian Institution

ABOUT THE EXHIBITION

"Beauty, Honor, and Tradition: The Legacy of Plains Indian Shirts" was organized by the National Museum of the American Indian, Smithsonian Institution, in collaboration with The Minneapolis Institute of Arts, in an effort to offer new perspectives on a historically and culturally important subject. As exhibition curators—one from each institution—we have brought different insights to the project, exploring relationships among the shirts, the shirtmakers, the historians and scholars, and the audience of Indians and non-Indians alike.

Shirts worn by Plains Indian men have long fascinated observers both within and outside Native America. Non-Natives and Natives alike admire the beauty of these shirts and the remarkable skill of the women who made them. Plains Indians, however, recognize the shirts' power, their deep cultural meaning, and the importance of the people who wore them. Each shirt was created to honor an individual and the deeds associated with him. Some shirts were also thought to hold intrinsic spiritual power, which was then transferred to the garment's owner or wearer. Among many tribes on the northern Plains, specific shirts were associated with medicine bundles; during medicine bundle ceremonies, the owner of the bundle would wear its corresponding shirt. These relationships between owners and shirts are significant. Likewise, Indians prize the shirts' craftsmanship and the relationships between the shirt-wearer and all those who helped make his shirt.

Many people, too, have contributed to creating this narrative. As curators, we agreed that it was important to make every effort to include all their voices in the exhibition and catalogue. Our first priority was to be true to the collective voice of the Indian people themselves: it is essential that people hear the voices of the shirtmakers' and -wearers' descendants. They relate the stories of the shirts, and explain how generations have continued the tradition of honoring exceptional people within their culture. We have also tried to include here the voices of scholarly research regarding specific shirts and their themes. The last voices are our own—those of two Native American curators who have cultural and academic knowledge of the shirts.

One difficulty with such a project is how to organize the shirts into a format that promotes an overall understanding of them, while providing insights into specific themes or examples. When other people have written about Plains Indian shirts, they have often organized the subject by style or construction, geographic region, or time frame. We have opted not to view the shirts chronologically. In part, this is because many of the shirts were created during a single forty-year period, and it is misleading to put in order styles that emerged on different parts of the Plains simultaneously. Chronological presentations of cultural material have also been interpreted to imply an evolution from less accomplished or complex to more so over time. In reality, these shirts represent the ingenuity of individual artists at specific times and under certain conditions, using the materials that were available to them. Finally, in chronological order, contemporary material is always shown last, and one of the most important points we wish to make is that shirts of honor on the Plains transcend time.

Instead, we decided to take a thematic approach. First, we analyzed more than four hundred shirts from the collections of the National Museum of the American Indian for their beauty, cultural significance, and emotional impact—perhaps the most difficult quality to judge. Once we had chosen the shirts for the exhibition, we began to place them into categories. Those categories will be examined in further detail later in this catalogue, but, to give one example, we felt that tribal style was an important topic to explore. Based on the extensive number of shirts in this collection from the Crow people, we set aside a section for them. We also knew many warrior–artists painted stories of their battle exploits on their shirts and wore them proudly. We wanted to examine this tradition of pictographic shirts, so we created a separate place for them as well.

In this format, when the exhibition is shown in New York and Minneapolis, the curator and the exhibition designer can rearrange the order of the categories, if they wish to, and still tell the story. Of course, we worked within certain limitations. First, there were several shirts in the collection that would have contributed to the exhibition but that had to be withdrawn because they are too fragile to display. In any case, we had the space and other resources to exhibit only a part of the holdings of the National Museum of the American Indian. Regrettably, the exhibition and book do not include shirts from every Plains tribe.

Finally, we traveled to Montana and South Dakota to interview Indian people about this material. We visited Native Americans living on Crow, Northern Cheyenne, Blackfeet, and Lakota reservations. Many individuals contributed immeasurably to this work. Too often museums have researched or exhibited Native American culture without visiting Native people. Tribal people should always be consulted about the presentation of their history and lives. We are pleased that they have a strong presence here.

We hope you are able to sense their presence, as well as the presence of their ancestors, who created this beautiful art.

THE LEGACY OF PLAINS INDIAN SHIRTS

These spectacular shirts, proudly worn by our ancestors, are a bridge connecting us to the past. Earned through acts of bravery, decorated in honor of great deeds, reflecting the deepest spiritual beliefs of the people who made and wore them, they are the closest we are ever going to get to our forefathers.

These shirts also represent an important period in our history. Their changing materials and tailoring record the arrival of new influences on the Plains—from white traders carrying glass beads and woven cloth, to relocated tribes bringing Eastern Woodlands artistic traditions, to U.S. Army soldiers dressed in their own style of war shirt. Ironically, despite all the images of Indians—especially Plains Indians—in American popular culture, this history is not well known. Little about our way of life is.

Scholars estimate that when Columbus arrived on these shores, more than five million people were living in what is now the United States. Assaulted by soldiers and settlers, and ravaged by the diseases they carried, our population plummeted to only 250,000 by the early 1900s. Government and Christian schools sought to erase our beliefs. Forced onto reservations, our land taken away and way of life destroyed, we were no longer seen stereotypically as threats to European-Americans, but rather as curiosities and aberrations, strangers in our own land.

Our family, like many others, has been active in trying to correct this sad fact by gathering and sharing knowledge of our culture. We take part in tribal celebrations and sacred ceremonies. Over the years our search for identity and ancestry has led us to the museums, because they house a large number of our cultural objects. Within these objects are our ancestors' lives, beauty, accomplishment, ability, pride, and power. We are especially blessed to be a father and son working together on this book and exhibition, which we hope will teach people about a part of Indian history and art.

PLAINS LIFE

As recently as 150 years ago, Plains Indian life followed the buffalo herds. Almost everything our people depended upon came from these wonderful, shaggy beasts. Their flesh provided food. Their hides provided clothing and shelter. Their dried bones became brushes; their horns—spoons; their hooves—bells and glue; their tendons—sinew used for sewing.

In the fall, the people would conduct massive hunts in which they obtained large amounts of meat. They sliced the meat and rinsed it with salt water and herbs, then smoked and dried it to eat in winter. When the snow began to fly, and grass on the prairies became scarce, the buffalo herds would separate into smaller groups, seeking the protected areas in the valleys by the rivers. There they would hunker down to survive the bitter winters. In spring, when the grass grew thick and tall on the Plains, the buffalo left the valleys behind and moved out onto the prairies. Massive herds of thousands of buffalo came together to breed and be nourished.

Although they hunted other animals as well, the Indian people fashioned the cycle of their year to match the buffalo's. The tribes, too, broke up into smaller groups during the winter and sought protection in the valleys. In the spring, like the buffalo, these small groups would rejoin each other. Tribes would then have ceremonies and socialize.

Most everything in the Plains Indian world, from the tiny awl to the towering tipi, is decorated in some manner. Winter was a time for creating this utilitarian art, spring and summer, a time to show it off. On the Plains, the making of artwork was divided up by gender. Women made most of the clothing and household things and created abstract decorations, while men made religious objects and painted realistic designs.

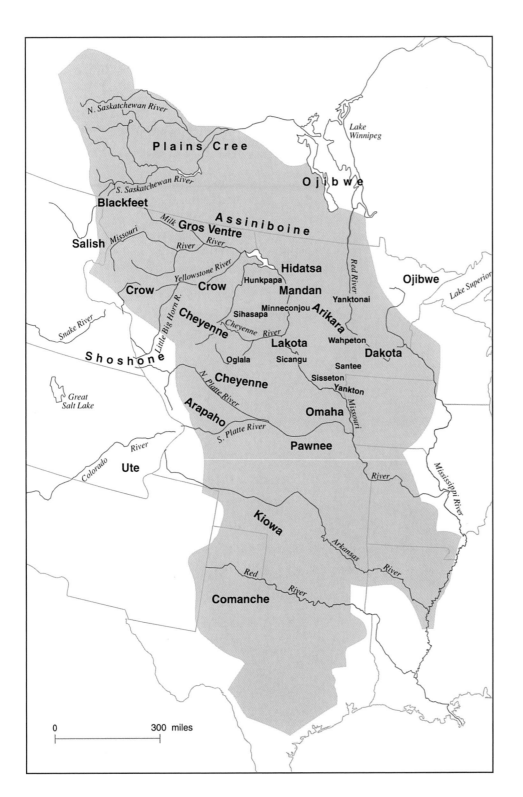

MAP OF THE
NORTH AMERICAN PLAINS

15

SHIRT MAKING

Although petroglyphs carved at sites such as Writing-On-Stone, in southern Alberta, record Plains Indian figures wearing fringed war shirts and leggings, the shirt tradition in the northern Plains is not an ancient one (Keyser 1996, 32). The explorer Maximilian, the artist George Catlin, the writer Alice Marriott, and other observers from the early part of the nineteenth century record that only a few Plains Indian men wore shirts. On his epic trip along the Missouri River from 1832 to 1834, Maximilian said of the Numakiki (Mandan) Indian people, "Even in the midst of winter the Mandan wore nothing on the upper part of their body" (Taylor 1980, 16–17; Maximilian 1906, 262). The Swiss artist Karl Bodmer, who accompanied Maximilian, recorded the likenesses of many northern Plains men; a vast majority of them are wrapped in robes, worn with the fur side in, while a few wear shirts covered with robes (Goetzmann 1984, 239, et al.).

A painted robe collected by Lewis and Clark in 1803 or 1804 is well executed, indicating that the tradition had been in place for a long period of time. By the 1830s, as Bodmer's watercolors show, decorative representations on robes had become more detailed and realistic. Plains shirts probably evolved from painted robes, though the two were also used simultaneously.

Research of museum collections all over the world indicates that the tribes who commonly wore shirts are the Inunaina (Arapaho); Piegan; Blood; Pikuni or Siksika (Blackfeet); Plains Cree; Apsaalooke (Crow); Nakoda (Assiniboine); A'aninin (Gros Ventre); Minitari, Numakiki, and Sahnish (Hidatsa, Mandan, and Arikara); Tsethasetas (Cheyenne); Teton Lakota; Sarci; and Wind River Shoshone. The tribes that less commonly used the shirt are the Plains Ojibwa, Chaticks Si Chaticks (Pawnee), Sisseton, and Yanktonai. The Ponca, Omaha, and Iowa used shirts occasionally (Taylor 1980, 19). People should use caution, however, in generalizing about shirts, especially when studying museum collections, as museums usually specialize in the spectacular rather than the average examples.

Buffalo hide is too thick and heavy to use for shirts, so shirtmakers used the skins of other animals. Elk provides a large hide, and deerskin is suitable as well. Antelope are plentiful, but their hides are small and thin. The ideal hides came from the abundant mountain sheep, which ranged from the Rocky Mountains to the Missouri River and beyond. The fact that these sheep, living high in the mountains, were difficult to hunt without guns made their hides especially valuable.

The hide was saved when the animal was butchered. Horns could be carved and bent into spoons or vessels, but the hide was the main attraction. The best skins were large, lightweight, and porous. When tanned properly, a process utilizing the animal's brains and liver, the hide became soft and supple. After scraping the inside of the hide clean, the tanner removed the hair as well. Often on the older, more classical shirts, an edge of hair was left on the bottom and the tail, too, was left intact. This narrow line of hair may have been left to strengthen that delicate thin edge. Now it is a way to identify older pieces, the so-called untailored shirt type.

The two hides then were placed, inside to inside, as if the deer were standing on its back legs. To form sleeves, each hide was cut in two, a bit behind the front legs, and folded and fitted on each side, leaving the bottom portion of the hide for the main body of the shirt. Thus, leg skins hung down from the bottom of the shirt as well as from the sleeves. When a shirt is made

17

this way, you can see in it the original shape of the hides; the animal's integrity is maintained in the shirt, and with it the animal's power. Once the hides were in position they were stitched together.

This early, classic form resembles a poncho, with the wearer's head fitting through the hole and the shirt draping gracefully downward. Few, if any, tie straps were used under the arms or sides to hold the shirt together, allowing maximum flow and freedom.

The skins of a woman's dress were oriented in the opposite way. In this case, the animal stands on its front legs, with its neck skin hanging down to form most of the central hemline. The gaps between this piece and the leg skins on either side were often filled with woven wool inserts. The hindquarters' skin was folded out and down to form a yoke. The front and back were identical, with the tail centered on the yoke. The dress was then sewn from the neck hole down the sleeves and from the underarm area down the sides.

For the dress, the hair side is inside, both front and back. Dresses were not painted, so a smooth outer surface wasn't necessary. When a dress inevitably became soiled, the nappy, fuzzy surface on the outside could be cleaned using a rough, pumice-like stone to sandpaper the hide until the soiled fibers were removed. The dress then could be touched up with some soft, white, chalk-like material.

As early as the 1830s, shirtmakers began experimenting with new design ideas. The skin legs that had hung from the cuffs and hem, for example, were discarded and the sleeves and sides enclosed. Many aspects of Indian culture eroded under the continued onslaught of European-Americans, and shirt styles were no exception. The change was not abrupt, but rather it was gradual. Because the northern Plains were more remote than the southern Plains, certain traditions lasted longer there, but even so, eventually change did come.

DECORATION

Once a shirt was constructed, it could be decorated in several different ways. Four strips of quillwork or beadwork could be attached to it: two extending over the shoulders and hanging midway down the back and the front; the other two attached to the sleeves, abutting the shoulder strips. The anthropologist Clark Wissler maintains that the placement of the strips depended upon the location of the seams, as they were meant to conceal them (Wissler, 1916:102). Among our tribe, the A'aninin (Gros Ventre), this style dates to the time of buffalo robes. Our people tanned the hides for making robes during the winter when the hide hair was lush and thick. The process took place in the tipi. When tanned, the two halves were reattached, but the sewing left a long, noticeable scar of a seam. To overcome this unsightliness, the makers devised a long strip of decorated hide to be sewn over the seam. At first, this strip was decorated with colorful designs made with embroidered, dyed porcupine quills, then later, with beads. Even after wool blankets commonly replaced animal hides, people customized them in keeping with the old traditions, with decorations known as blanket strips.

Neck tabs or facings, both front and back, are also seen on Plains shirts. Some tribes preferred square-shaped tabs, while others employed pointed tabs or other shapes. Rosettes are often found on the early shirts, in the middle of the chest and back. Lush hair, from humans or horses, often extends back from the quilled arm strips and down and outside of the shoulder strips. Shirts with hair have been called scalp shirts, but the hair bundles are only hair locks. Also decorating these same areas can be long lengths of fringe. They give a flowing motion, a luxuriant richness to the composition of the shirt.

Another old technique of decorating war shirts consists of cutting holes out of the material in patterns that are both beautiful and symbolic. The rows of holes can make an X across the chest or down the length of the sleeve. It is not unusual to see patterns of slices through the material on the main trunk of the body, in the elbow area or elsewhere. Such alterations contribute to the overall aesthetics of the garment. The style may have originated among people living along the Columbia River and spread eastward among the Flathead, Pikuni or Siksika (Blackfeet), A'aninin (Gros Ventre), and Apsaalooke (Crow) Indian people. Some tribes incorporated such shirts into their religious practices. They were called bear shirts among the early Blackfeet because the holes were thought to have been made by bear. It was believed that people wearing these shirts had the power of that animal. (See page 39.)

PAINTED SHIRTS

A shirt could also be filled with vivid color. Pictographic artwork, in particular, painted on tipis and shields, as well as robes and shirts, accommodated the warrior tradition. These paintings record the brave and successful exploits of individual men. On certain robes you can see early Plains artwork at its finest. Painting hides was a precise endeavor. The powdered pigments came from many sources: the earth, plants, and even animals. A pale red earth pigment could be found on the sides of cliffs in the Bear Paw Mountains in Montana. A deeper red came from caves near Helena, Montana, and yellow from Northern Cheyenne country, buffalo gall-stones, and wolf-moss. Pulverized coal could produce black. Red, yellow, and blue were the preferred hues. A wide variety of colors could be obtained from the countryside as the people became more familiar with nature's bounty.

Carved buffalo bones of various shapes served as the brushes. The more porous sections of the hipbones carried a lot of paint and could be shaped into a fine blade that produced a thin line, or they could be left with a rounded edge that made a wider stroke. The end of a frayed willow could tint a wide area, and various lengths of willow served as measuring devices.

The inner membrane of a hide, when boiled, produced a type of glue or sizing, as did the juice of the cactus. When mixed with pigments this sizing would bind them together, making bright and durable paint. Or the painter could apply pigment directly to the shirt, then brush sizing over it, like varnish, to seal it.

19

With everything ready, the artist dipped the bone brush into the paint. The artist began by carefully making an outline of the desired form, because once the pigments touched the surface of the hide, their colors were absorbed and became part of it. At this point there was no erasing a mistake. Soon the drawing took form. Each stroke had to be painted somewhat gradually, to blend with the line made by the strokes before and after it. The paint-filled bone pressed the color into the soft, tanned skin rather than just covering its surface. Other colors applied between the painted outlines completed the work.

Painted robes were usually worn with the animal head on the left. As we now study the robes, we notice that the pictures usually flow in the same direction, from right to left. The scene depicted is usually of a battle in which the wearer and his tribe are victorious. There may be a series of vignettes showing various activities. Usually the paintings include a large number of people and horses. The animals' hoof prints covering the robe show the horses are running. Looking at the most detailed and colorful robes, you can almost hear the blast of the musket, the thundering of hooves, and the screams of the horses. You can almost smell the smoke and feel the dust of the encounter. Because these are battle scenes, the paintings show the dead as well as the living.

A good artist depicts minute details. By studying Plains Indian art you can often determine what tribes are depicted by their hairstyle or their moccasins or other accoutrements. You can identify the military societies to which they belonged by their regalia or shield patterns. A very detailed robe may be historically encyclopedic, although there is no absolute and final interpretation of it. The wearer may have asked his friends to help him paint the battle as a testimony to him and his fellow warriors. By inviting other artists to assist him, he was striving for historical accuracy.

The subjects in such a painting are usually presented in a flat, abstract style. Horses could be green, red, yellow, or any color. The artist is saying, "These are horses of many colors." A pinto doesn't have to have neat curvilinear spots; even by showing geometric spots, the artist is telling you, "This is a pinto." If you look at these shirts closely, you can see that the spots were often made with the artist's thumb or fingerprint. In other scenes on very early hides the artist has painted the rider in a way that shows both of his legs. The horse is not transparent, but rather this is a stylistic representation to show the rider mounted on the horse. Very early paintings show horses with hooked hooves; this may be a way to show that the hoof is not cloven. A painted robe is not a photograph, but it tells a story in beautiful color with plenty of action.

Such a recording of a great battle, one that may have saved the tribe, also demonstrated to the youngsters what it meant to be a warrior and visually encouraged them to achieve this level of accomplishment.

While pictographic robes usually recorded great battles, victories, and the exploits of their wearers, other types of illustrated robes evolved as well. For example, the Box and Border motif represents a special ceremony for a young girl, and the so-called Sunburst pattern represents a war bonnet, a symbol of pride and honor.

So in addition to looking attractive, painted robes are adventure books, recording the great accomplishments of tribal heroes. We want to stress here that the pictographs on robes and shirts served as mnemonic devices within the oral tradition of the Plains tribes. They are a kind of visual language, a language a shirt's owner could consult to tell the story of his deeds and one we can learn to read as well.

Quillwork and Beadwork

Porcupine quills were used in early decorations. In our tribe it is forbidden to kill a porcupine, because, as our grandmother and great-grandmother told us, "They are easy to kill, so we must save them for the hard times." Instead, quills were obtained by striking the live porcupine with coarse wet material, which would snag the quills and pull them out (today, most quills are gathered from porcupines found dead along the roadside). The quills were washed to rid them of oil, then etched in a solution that left the surface slightly irregular so the dye could take hold. The complex art of quillworking resembles a flat weave.

While working, the quillworker kept the quills in her mouth so the warm saliva could soften them. Two threads or pieces of sinew were used to sew parallel lines on the base material upon which the quills were folded. As the artist removed each quill from her mouth, she flattened it with her teeth. One end of the quill was then tucked under the sinew or thread, laid across the base material, and wrapped over the thread on the opposite side. When wrapped properly, the quills lay crossways forming a lane of color. The next row would go alongside. This simple method became complicated as more quills were added, and the end result is incredibly beautiful. In the completed work, no holes extend through the material and no threads are visible. All one sees are the linear porcupine quills tightly sewn down. When the strips were completed, they were attached to the shirt. If any damage occurred to the shirt, the strips could be removed and put on another shirt.

In the early 1800s, glass beads, usually manufactured in Venice, Italy, appeared on the Great Plains. These, too, were used to decorate shirt strips, eventually replacing quillwork. It is said that traders on ponies brought the first beads to the Plains, so they were called pony beads. They were fairly large, ranging up to an eighth of an inch in diameter. The first beads were primarily blue, red, black, and white; many tribes preferred the blue.

Sometime after 1840, seed beads made their way out to Indian country. Although they were smaller than pony beads, the Indian people preferred them for their wide variety of colors. These beads were easily obtained and adaptable to traditional quill patterns. There are two basic methods to apply beads: the appliqué stitch and the lazy stitch. The appliqué method usually involves two sinews or threads: one thread is strung with beads of the desired color and laid flat and sewn to the hide or cloth at close intervals with the second. In the lazy stitch, five or six beads are strung on a thread and the same thread is used to sew them to the material. The following rows are sewn parallel, like railroad ties. The rows will eventually bulge up forming a washboard pattern, adding texture to the surface. By selecting pleasing color schemes, great artwork is produced. Some tribes prefer one method to the other, a helpful bit of knowledge for tribal identification. For example, Sioux artists prefer the lazy stitch while the Blackfeet use the appliqué stitch.

Creative Indian people decorated shirts in many different ways. But every time someone believes they have seen all such designs, another beautiful garment surfaces, revealing a completely new method. Studying these shirts is a rewarding adventure.

WARRIORS

It is important to remember, however, that these shirts are more than a wonderful art form. They represent a difficult period of history on the American Plains, and the spiritual response of Plains Indian people to a dangerously shifting world.

In long-ago days, Plains Indians organized themselves by relationships into tribes, each coming to share a common culture. These tribes pursued their livelihood wherever it might lead. While traveling, they often met other groups, and these encounters could be confrontational. To protect themselves and assure their people's survival, each tribe developed a class of soldiers called warriors. In many tribes, male children joined age-graded societies where they learned cooperation and developed the strength, endurance, and skills necessary for warfare. As they got older, they moved on to more sophisticated societies, always working toward adulthood when they would become warriors.

Protecting their tribe and assuring its survival were the foremost responsibilities of these warriors. Encounters between tribes weren't always contentious. In fact, many tribes formed alliances. But inevitably there would be disputes. Then a tribe's warriors might defend their people's camp from attack, or they might carry the action into the field or to the enemy's camp.

Successful warriors received great honor, gained much esteem, and elevated their position within the tribe. Younger boys looked up to them as heroes, and wanted to become warriors and achieve fame, too. The warrior culture ensured that Plains tribes would always have a steady supply of defenders.

One acknowledgment and reward for great military deeds earned by successful warriors was the privilege of wearing specially made shirts and leggings that proclaimed their accomplishments and lofty status. But fighting with the invaders did not always provide the answers for peace. New times called for new skills, in politics and diplomacy. So many of the older, proven warriors—men like the Lakota statesman Red Cloud—negotiated with the white government either locally or in Washington, D.C. These negotiators, too, often dressed in their warrior shirts, symbols of their abilities and achievements.

CONTEMPORARY INDIAN SHIRTS

At the end of the nineteenth century, as the buffalo neared extinction and our families were placed on reservations, political and cultural survival became increasingly important. Triumph on the battlefield was no longer crucial to everyday life. These changes meant, too, that Native materials became scarce, and trade materials more abundant. Reservation Indians began to wear trousers and tailored shirts. For ceremonies and celebrations, our great-grandparents wore cloth shirts with flared cuffs and brightly colored ribbons emblazoned on their chests and arms. You can see the influence of this new style in the ribbon shirts worn by dancers, and just about everyone else, at Indian celebrations today.

In some ways, during the first decades of the twentieth century, reservation Indians lived much like other Americans on farms and in small towns. In other ways, their lives were very different. For example, Native Americans weren't recognized as citizens in our own country until the Indian Citizenship Act was passed on June 2, 1924. Poverty was the result of the severely restricted opportunities and resources available on reservations, and continues to plague our communities even to this day.

That was a time when it wasn't popular to be an Indian. But on the reservation there is very little choice, so our parents and grandparents periodically observed their tribal customs. Things that once were part of everyday life began to center on community celebrations called powwows. Every community had at least one such large annual festival, where special activities like presenting an Indian name to a child, celebrating a child's first dance, or holding a give-away memorial for a deceased relative took place in front of the entire tribe. These things take place at powwows today.

In the early 1900s, with the evolution of the religious Crow Belt Dance into the secular Grass Dance, proper attire at powwows became important. Men usually wore a roach or head-dress (not the feathered war bonnet), a cloth shoulder yoke, decorated moccasins, and fetlocks around their ankles. These last were made of wool or mop-like strands wrapped around a dyed pair of long underwear. Over this layer, the men wore ankle bells, and a belt and britch cloth secured around the waist. Photographs of this era show active people having a great time. Here and there you can see a shirt made in the old way. To this day among Plains Indians, it is still important to wear the proper attire for dancing. Women must have a shawl, which they place over their shoulders to qualify them to dance. Men must have a more elaborate outfit. And even if we wear quieter shirts—shirts that speak in a whisper, compared to the shirts of our ancestors—they are still beautiful.

23

In 1945, when the Indian warriors returned home after fighting for the United States in World War II, they told of all the wonderful things they saw and experienced while they were away, off the American Indian reservations. Later, many Indian veterans took their families to the cities to seek better lives. Change accelerated in the late 1960s, when Indian people became involved in the Civil Rights Movement. For many of us, this involvement began at Alcatraz in 1969. It was here that we recognized our own plight and realized that we had to become more active in order to change it. As we began to speak out, our speech took many forms. Huge photographic murals of Indian chiefs began to appear in public places, manifestations of Indian pride.

Young Indian people began to enroll in colleges in unprecedented numbers. T-shirts proclaimed, "Kiss Me I'm Indian," "Sitting Bull Lives!" or "Custer Had It Coming." Later, one featured Columbus's ships within a circle with a slash mark across it. These T-shirts are modern examples of clothing worn as a form of expression.

Today some of the warrior shirts of old are still in Indian hands, protected against theft and against the collectors who eagerly seek them. Other shirts are commissioned by various individuals for dancing or other purposes, and on rare occasions warrior shirts are inspired by visions. Although we have had to let go of many ancient ways under the onslaught of severe external forces, we continue to observe many customs to this very day, and will tomorrow. We are praying and seeking visions on mountaintops or fasting in the Sundance lodges. These are good signs. Our past is not so long ago, and important to our future.

On the Northern Cheyenne Indian Reservation in southern Montana, a tribal leader named Alonzo Spang worked very hard for years pursuing an academic course. Eventually he earned a Ph.D. In recognition of his achievement, his family and friends presented him with a warrior's war shirt and leggings—they extended an old way of honoring heroism to a new way of ensuring the well-being of their tribe. We are all proud of Dr. Spang.

In some Indian communities, recreation and sports are limited. But if there is a common unifier, it is basketball. People don't need complex, expensive machinery to play the game—just a ball and a hoop, and even those don't have to be fancy. Across Indian country, this interest in basketball starts at home and continues through grade school and beyond. It's a way to learn about teamwork and achieve honor. In high school, basketball is especially popular, and players have uniforms, cheerleaders, enthusiastic audiences, and statewide competitions, as many rural communities off the reservation place a high value on basketball competition, as well. In the year 2000, the Heart Butte High School on the Blackfeet Indian Reservation in northwest Montana won the state championship Class C Division basketball tournament. It was a wonderful and emotional time for many people in the community, and we were lucky enough to be there to talk with the coach and the team members about their victory. They were all very proud of themselves and their high school. They recognized their new status as role models for the younger children, and they realized they had achieved a greater level of responsibility. At the end of the interview, with cameras rolling, we asked the team to stand up, turn around, and show us the attractive war shirt jackets they earned. The back of each shirt was brightly emblazoned with the word "Champs"—American Indian warrior shirts in a new form.

It is important to note here that our work on this project also included listening to the oral traditions of Plains tribes from men and women who heard them from their grandparents and great-grandparents. The elders and other cultural representatives of the Crow, Northern Cheyenne, Blackfeet, and Lakota Indian people we visited on their reservations shared a lot of useful information with us. We hope their voices can be heard in this book.

Relatively few Plains war shirts survive in museum collections or private hands. Many were buried with their owners—that is how important they are, spiritually. Through art, color, and power, they embody the creativity, bravery, history, philosophy, and religion of the people who made and wore them. For us, they bring to life our ancestors' world, a place of beauty, honor, and tradition, made richer by the importance of family, pride, and The One Above. Working with them has been a joy and a great honor.

A SHIRT AND A PAIR OF LEGGINGS were the essential components of the full outfit of a mid-nineteenth-century northern Plains Indian warrior. The large quilled chest disk, rectangular chest pattern, pony beads, long extended neck tabs, and painted leggings are all stylistic hallmarks from this region and time period.

Large pony beads were the first glass beads imported into this region, quickly replacing traditional porcupine quills for decoration. The painted figures on the leggings probably represent bird tracks, in Blackfeet cosmology. The fringes on the leggings are locks of human hair; among Blackfeet these identify the wearer as a warrior who has taken scalps.

The fringes on some leggings and/or moccasins were so long and excessive that they would have made walking on the ground ungainly, so it is assumed these types of clothes were fabricated to be worn by an equestrian.

Pikuni or Siksika (Blackfeet)
Leggings, about 1850
Collection history: exchanged with Lewis C. G. Clarke
in London, England, and accessioned by NMAI in 1922.
11.1303

Pikuni or Siksika (Blackfeet)
Shirt (back), about 1850
Collection history: John Burling Lawrence collection,
obtained by his brother in 1860, and accessioned
into the NMAI collection in 1927.
15.3394

"And the garment war shirt is a very special garment to the individual that owns it. They don't wear it every day. Only on special occasions. Special ceremonies. . . . And before an individual becomes an outstanding chief, he's got to accomplish so many [kinds of] particular requirements."

JOHN HILL (APSAALOOKE)

CERTAIN SPECIAL PEOPLE in the American Indian world possess power. This force can emanate from various sources: divine birth, profound spirituality, extraordinary strength and physical abilities, superlative performance as a warrior, brilliant leadership, a close interaction with The One Above, or combinations of these sources. This power forms and directs its possessors' lives and things around them. Possessing some degree of power is vital to survival, but possessing many powers makes a person extraordinary.

According to tribal oral traditions, powerful people frequently demonstrated their abilities. Items associated with such people often changed from the ordinary to the extraordinary. The places where they lived became special; their tipis, shields, and ceremonial objects gained force. Shirts, however, amalgamated more power than anything else. Both the religious and the physical aspects of shirts contributed to this power.

A man who wore a shirt probably owned more than one shirt over his lifetime. As a young man gained warrior status, his honors increased along with his abilities and accomplishments. Eventually the more powerful warriors evolved into statesmen or medicine men. The shirts they wore as they reached these various stages of power tell their stories and bear witness to their deeds. Occasionally we can deduce the specific identity of the original owner of an existing shirt. More often these shirts must be seen to represent all ancestral shirt wearers. When in the presence of these shirts, some sensitive observers can often feel a warmth or energy emanating from them. This is the glow from the power the shirt still holds.

Students of Indian war shirts should recognize that the garments are a culmination of collaborative efforts. First, the hunter obtained the skin from his relative, the deer. Next, the deer hide was tanned, fashioned, and decorated with quillwork or beadwork by a prominent woman in his life, usually his wife. Then the owner decorated the shirt as well, painting and drawing accounts of the deeds that protected his tribe. When a warrior was dressed in his shirt, he embodied a level of beauty, achievement, and ability that inspired others to emulate him.

Active warriors accomplishing heroic deeds perspired within their shirts. The porous shirt easily absorbed the salty sweat, causing the man and his shirt to become united. So, while the shirt is a combination of the skills of many, its interior surface embodies the physical testimony of the man who wore it, evidenced by its wear and coloration. In this way, the shirts almost take on a life or presence of their own. They are our ancestors, and when we are near them they unite us with our forefathers and what they represent. This is power.

29

This shirt, decorated with a style of quillwork very rarely seen, belonged to the noted Lakota Chief Sinte Gleska (Spotted Tail), who was born during the winter of 1823 and died 58 years later on what is now Rosebud Indian Reservation in South Dakota. Sinte Gleska's life is a symbol of tribal perseverance through very difficult times for Plains Indian people.

As a young man, Sinte Gleska became a shirt wearer by successfully leading a war party. It is said that Sinte Gleska's shirt was adorned with more than a hundred locks of hair, representing coups, scalps, and captured horses.

During unrest between the Lakota and the U.S. military, Sinte Gleska offered himself to the U.S. authorities in exchange for Lakota women and children who were being held prisoner. While imprisoned at Ft. Leavenworth, he learned some English and studied the ways of the European-Americans. After his release, Sinte Gleska joined peace delegations to Washington, D.C. He believed that his people must be educated in the manner of European-Americans in order to survive in the new world. Thus, he sent his sons to the Carlisle Indian School in Pennsylvania for a Western education. When his sons came home for a visit, Sinte Gleska was disappointed to learn they were being trained for the U.S. military. He withdrew his children from the school and demanded that a new school be erected on his people's lands. Today, Sinte Gleska University, the first tribal college on Rosebud Indian Reservation, honors the name of this respected chief (Termin).

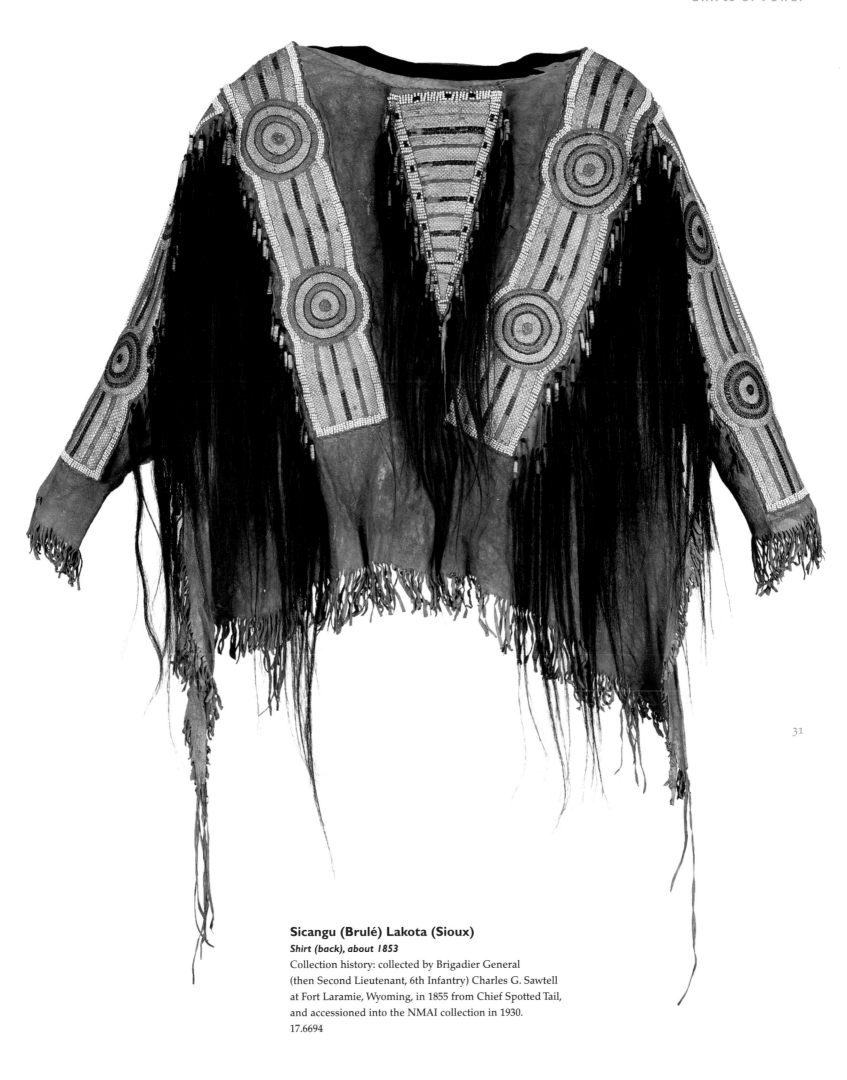

Sicangu (Brulé) Lakota (Sioux)
Shirt (back), about 1853
Collection history: collected by Brigadier General
(then Second Lieutenant, 6th Infantry) Charles G. Sawtell
at Fort Laramie, Wyoming, in 1855 from Chief Spotted Tail,
and accessioned into the NMAI collection in 1930.
17.6694

The quill strips on this exceptional shirt were made using a multi-quill, oblique plaiting technique that creates diamond shapes in three colors: pink, green, and yellow. Under close examination, the high level of artistry is a testament to the quillwork skills passed down through generations of women. Among the Cheyenne, only dedicated women are allowed to quill. Each woman is trained under close supervision by her mentor to ensure the quality of her work.

Tsethasetas (Cheyenne)
Shirt (back), about 1885
Collection history: collected by General Nelson A. Miles
and presented by Mrs. Samuel K. Reber and Major Sherman Miles
to the museum. Accessioned into the NMAI collection in 1925.
14.2245

Plains Indian shirts can be extraordinarily beautiful, as this one is. Each shirt has several stories to tell. We can interpret, learn from, and enjoy some of these stories; others remain puzzling. This shirt speaks of tribal artists and great beauty.

The accession record states that this shirt may have been obtained from Sitting Bull, the great Lakota leader, and was collected in 1870 by A. E. Brooks. Material attributions from the past are not known for their accuracy, however, and, when incorrect, can create confusion and subsequent inaccuracies. It is highly improbable that Sitting Bull ever owned this shirt. Hundreds of items in public and private collections around the world have been connected to this famous warrior, but it is unlikely he owned all of them. The record also states that the Nez Perce people of Idaho made this shirt. Scholars argue that most shirts of this type originated with the Crow people. A Crow woman artist probably created this shirt in the first quarter of the nineteenth century.

Research, Crow history, and the Crow Indian material itself show that Crow artists were trendsetters. Numerous examples of their superior artistic ability abound, and this shirt is one.

The lavish abundance of fringe on this shirt is immediately striking—can you imagine wearing it, with all of the flowing fringe following your every move?—such abundance is always an expression of wealth.

Next, notice the special type of quillwork on the decorative strips. The long, narrow rows of material are linear bundles of porcupine-quill-wrapped horsehair. This rare process is complex and detailed. A single bundle or two bundles of long horsehair are carefully wrapped in quills so none of the hair shows through except at the ends. The quills can be arranged by color to form patterns. The two bundles on this shirt were then sewn down the middle to a leather strip, and this strip was sewn to the shirt, creating a marvelous decoration.

We can image the artist stepping back from the deerskin palette and considering her fashionable creation. There may have been more empty space at the ends of the sleeves than she preferred, so she embellished them with rows of perforations. Finally, perhaps to render the work truly unique, she added a series of similar perforations between the neck and the back left torso.

Pikuni or Siksika (Blackfeet)
Shirt (back), about 1870
Collection history: collected by William Wildschut
at the Blackfeet Reservation, Montana, in 1925,
and accessioned into the NMAI collection in 1925.
14.3567

In order to remain alive, traditions must be able to endure change while maintaining their core values. War shirts have changed over the years and will continue to change as Native American communities and values adjust to contemporary American life. Today, achievement and the betterment of the community are still important, but Indian people no longer have to perform on battlefields; other fields of dedication and accomplishment have replaced them.

A key to survival in today's Indian world is education, and for many "warriors," male and female, schools have become the arena of achievement.

In many respects, life on Indian reservations is bleak, and residents usually live at the lower end of the economic scale. Yet early in 2000, the Heart Butte High School on the Blackfeet Indian Reservation in northwest Montana won the state basketball championship of the Class C division with a 26–0 record. The importance of achieving this honor can be found in the words of the victors themselves:

"Everyone dedicated themselves, coming to practice, going hard and not getting mad at each other. We had really good communication. We knew how to play."

"[We gave up a lot of things to practice and play, like] going out with your friends on weekends and stuff. After school, you have to go to practice."

"It was all worth it. Yeah. I had to drop the girlfriends . . . yeah."

"It felt pretty good because we had the elders there [at Browning, another town on the reservation] talking to us, praying over us. And it felt good going away protected. It gives you a lot of confidence when the elder people start noticing."

"[When we won we had a] victory dance. It was awesome, because you don't really get to see many things like that [anymore]. So, we came back . . . it was a first for me, doing a victory dance and stuff. We had elders here, we had people in their buckskins and [war bonnets] and stuff. Pretty neat."

Those are the changing forms of the continuing tradition of war shirts.

HEART BUTTE

WARRIORS
26-0
STATE
CLASS "C"
CHAMPS
'2000'

41

Pikuni or Siksika (Blackfeet)
Heart Butte Basketball Jacket (back), 2000
Blackfeet Indian Reservation, Heart Butte,
Montana

"We live in the tradition that one is judged as being a success by how much they have done for the people. . . . We live in the tradition where what we have done for others, in service of our people, is what really counts."
BURTON PRETTY ON TOP (APSAALOOKE)

ALMOST EVERY OBJECT in traditional Plains Indian society was decorated, reflecting both a personal style and a tribal aesthetic. Objects that were made for children were beautifully decorated as well. Lakota quillwork artist Christine Red Cloud illustrates the importance of these things:

> [The family] brought out this quilled baby bonnet, and it was old, but the colors were still real nice. They said that it had been handed down from family to family. [The tradition started when a white lady] was expecting and all the Indians were excited that she was expecting. [One of the Indian women] made the bonnet for the baby . . . a girl. So the Indians had a big dance, and then they gave the baby the bonnet. So ever since then, they've passed it from family to family. The quillwork itself is beautiful.

From the tiniest details on small items, to the more comprehensive decoration of larger things, Plains Indian people have demonstrated a keen aesthetic sense that empowers both the object and its owner. Shirts created for honored community members were carefully constructed and decorated. Most war shirts have common elements, such as beaded or quilled arm and chest bands, and hair locks that hang from the arms, designed to empower the shirts, but the extra details artisans incorporated into them make the shirts powerful to the observer's eye.

Hair locks or leather fringes were routinely attached to war shirts. These embodied personal power. Whether the hair was given to the shirt wearer by his family, taken from an enemy, or taken from an animal, locks were an embodiment of personal honor. Hair locks also added another layer of beauty to the shirt. When the shirt wearer rode his horse, the hair locks would undulate, creating a sense of power and presence.

Details such as painted designs and sewn-on ornaments give many shirts the appearance of extra power or strength. Although such details may or may not have had cultural significance, they can still be appreciated for their beauty.

43

The owner of this scalp shirt was probably the head chief of the Itazipcho (Sans Arc) Lakota, indicated by the blue and yellow colors of the paints. Among the Lakota, the Wicasa Yatapika, "shirt wearers," or head chiefs, were the only men who had the right to wear painted scalp shirts. Demonstrations of great sacrifice and bravery were required to earn this high rank in traditional Lakota society. Such chiefs were imbued with supernatural powers used to protect and serve their people (Powell, 48).

In battle, shirt wearers were the first to charge and the last to depart. If a comrade's horse was shot, leaving the warrior on foot, the shirt wearer was obliged to rescue him. If a shirt wearer did not fulfill his duties, he was stripped of the right to wear the sacred garment, and he and his family were humiliated.

The scalp locks on this shirt symbolize the shirt wearer's deeds and dedication to his people. The two primary colors, blue and yellow, symbolize the sky and rock, basic elements of the Lakota cosmos. The three-dotted decorative pattern could represent a celestial constellation, or the track of an animal important to the shirt's owner.

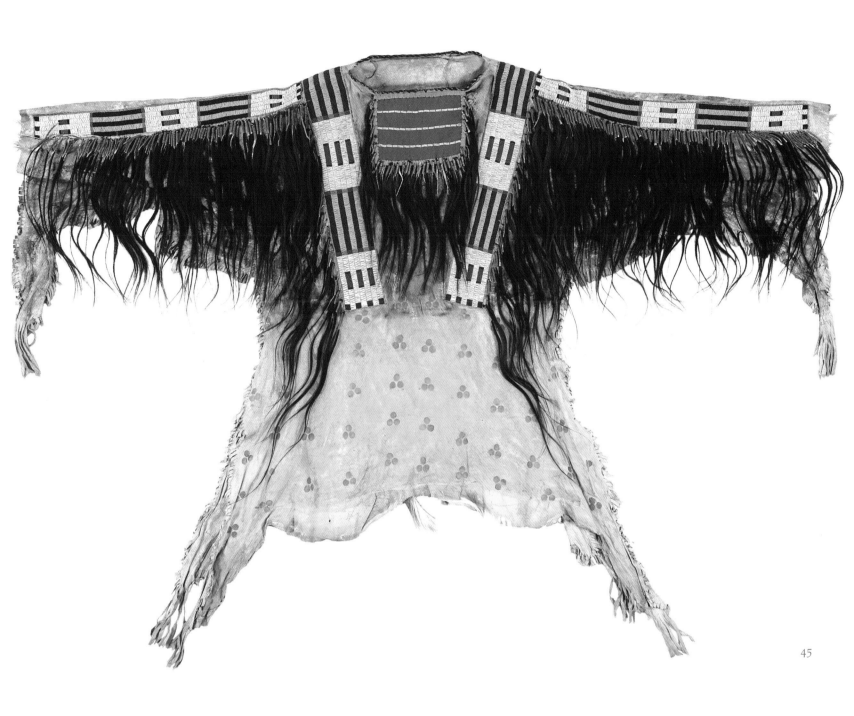

45

Itazipcho (Sans Arc) Lakota (Sioux)
Shirt (back), about 1870
Collection history: Stephen Jewett collection
accessioned by NMAI in 1907.
01.3920

This strong war shirt has hair locks on the arms. The beaded strips are crafted in classic Blackfeet style, with large, stepped triangle patterns filled with layers of color. The surface painting is also executed in a characteristic Blackfeet style. This includes black, oval-shaped designs, each with a single black zigzag line radiating from the bottom, unique to Blackfeet shirts and leggings. There have been several interpretations of this design. One version holds that the ovals symbolize tadpoles (Taylor, 1993, 65). The changing nature of the frog is important in traditional Blackfeet stories. Some contemporary Blackfeet elders contend that this design represents a scalp with hair, which would enhance the hair locks that adorn the sleeves and body of this shirt—the combination of real hair locks attached to the shirt and painted ones would emphasize the warrior's bravery in battle and his ability to overcome enemies.

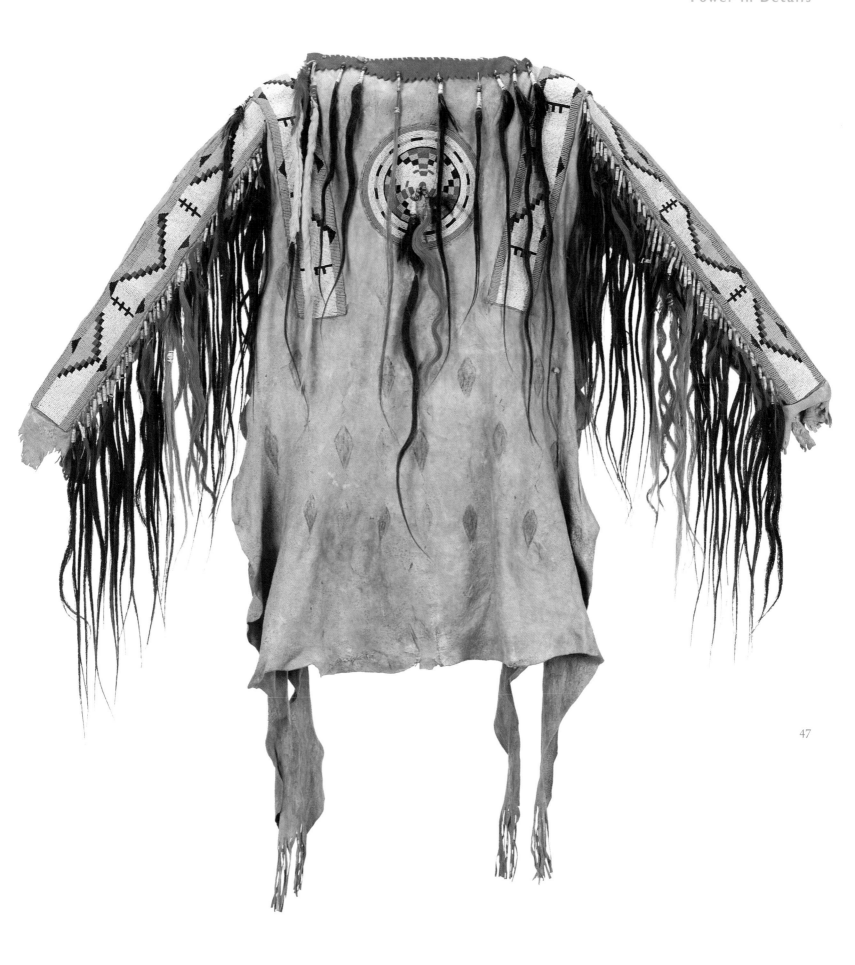

47

Pikuni or Siksika (Blackfeet)

Shirt (back), about 1880

Collection history: Keppler collection, accessioned by NMAI in 1906.

00.8904

48

This beautifully quilled and painted shirt features leather fringe complemented with dyed horsehair. Like the other shirts in this section, its quillwork style and construction are similar to those made by the Mandan, Hidatsa, and Arikara tribes. It was probably traded to the Assiniboine.

**Numakiki, Sahnish, or Minitari
(Mandan, Arikara, or Hidatsa)**

Shirt (back), about 1875

Collection history: collected from the Assiniboine at Wolf Point, Montana,
given to NMAI by De Cost Smith, and accessioned into the collection in 1939.
20.1456

This unusual shirt has beaded strips decorated with two different patterns; one set may have been transferred from another shirt or leggings. The main body of the shirt is probably older than the beaded strips. It has been painted with stripes and scalp-lock designs, a common Blackfeet convention most often found on older shirts.

The Blackfeet created and acquired shirts in a sacred manner. According to contemporary Blackfeet elders, a warrior would go out to the hills and fast for spiritual power to protect him in battle. This sacred rite enhanced the war shirt, giving the warrior great power.

When a Blackfeet warrior needed a war shirt, according to the elders, he would ask a highly skilled woman to create the beadwork. He directed her work because all elements of the shirt were significant to his own life. The painted horizontal bands represent the number of times he went to battle, and the beaded medallion on the chest symbolizes his enemy's village.

War shirts like this one were, and continue to be, considered sacred by the Blackfeet people. When a shirt was transferred from one owner to the next, the previous owner would be honored in a ceremony.

Pikuni (Blackfeet)
Shirt (back), about 1880
Collection history: collected at the Piegan Reservation, Southern Alberta,
Canada, by D. Cadzow, accessioned by NMAI in 1926.
14.9385

51

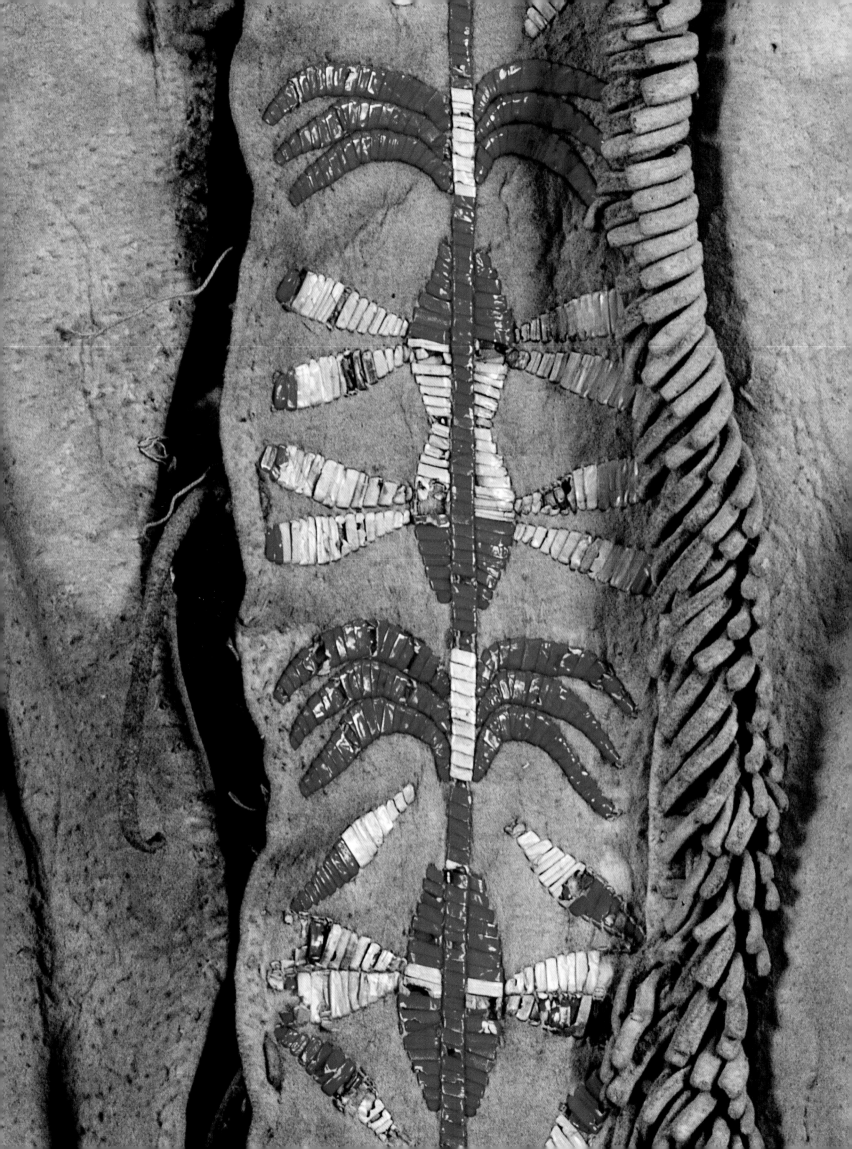

" . . . A weasel represents quick movement; [they] observe sharply, and [if they see]
anything moving, they're very quickly, in the twinkling of an eye, back into their
shelter. That's the . . . weasel. That's why they were tied to the war shirt."

DONALD STEWART (APSAALOOKE)

IN THE WARRIOR CULTURE of Plains Indian men during the 1700s, warriors found ways to record their battle deeds. These visual encyclopedias were recorded testimonies of exploits that would be one measure of a man's worth. Battles among Plains tribes were not intended to annihilate the enemy, but to defend themselves and their land, acquire honor, and amass wealth in the form of horses.

The arts were divided into two categories, with gender-specific roles. Plains Indian women concentrated their artistic efforts on decorating items with geometric designs. Some say these designs were chosen solely for their aesthetic value; others argue that, like many other aspects of Plains Indian art, geometric designs were probably abstract representations of long-ago stories.

Men's arts involved pictographic representations, either painted or drawn. They recorded battle exploits or visionary experiences. Mostly found on tipis and buffalo robes, and in ledgers, the pictographic style was also used on shirts. Not only did the drawings on a shirt recount the bravery of the shirt wearer and outline the events of a battle, they could also provide an opportunity for boasting.

Most Plains Indian pictographs remaining today are not attributed to specific warrior–artists. The earliest known Plains Indian artist is Mato-Tope (Four Bears), who befriended two fellow painters who visited the Plains in the early 1830s. Both American artist George Catlin and Swiss artist Karl Bodmer remarked that Mato-Tope was a gifted artist and a great chief of his people, the Mandan. During the winter of 1833–34, Bodmer spent many hours with the noted chief and gave him gifts of paper, pencils, and watercolors (Maurer, 192). With these tools, Mato-Tope seamlessly transferred his warrior–artist style paintings on traditional materials into new media.

Bodmer portrayed Mato-Tope wearing a pictographic shirt, thereby contributing to the recorded history of pictographs. Like other traditional Plains Indian artists, Mato-Tope developed his own personal style of depicting figures and horses.

Early pictographs, painted first on robes and then on shirts, show figures rendered with minimal features. When accompanied by the story of the exploit, the drawings served as a mnemonic device; explicit features were not needed since they would be described in the detailed narrative. As newer materials became available and inter-tribal trade increased, drawing and painting styles began to change. Figures began to be shown with distinguishable hairstyles, detailed clothing, and weapons. Drawings of horses also became stylized, reflecting diverse artistic traditions across the Plains.

Scenes most commonly recorded on pictographic shirts are exploits of counting coup and horse raiding, two greatly honored endeavors. These shirts, rich in artistic style and tradition, also symbolize Plains Indian people's efforts to preserve their way of life.

53

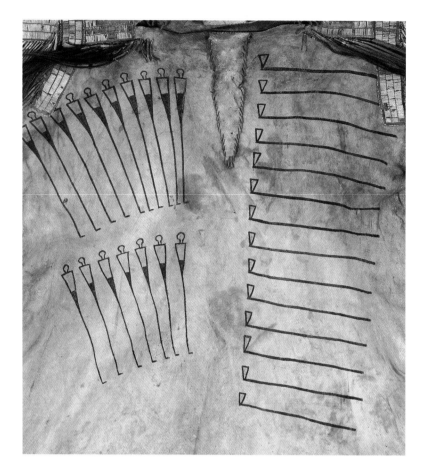

This shirt is one of the oldest in NMAI's collections. Its tailoring, ornamentation, and abstract painting are indicative of shirts Plains Indian men wore when Karl Bodmer traveled up the Missouri River in the 1830s. Its style and the museum's records indicate the shirt is Mandan.

Three components distinguish this example from later shirts. On each of the arms, the warrior–artist has painted black stripes; these contribute to the overall aesthetic of the shirt. Combined with the scalp locks, the stripes probably refer to the number of times he went into battle.

On the back of the shirt, the warrior–artist has painted, on the right side, fourteen wide horizontal bars ending with inverted triangles. These represent pipes. To carry a pipe during a war party was an honor reserved for men held in high regard within the community. Each wide bar is the stem of a pipe, and the triangle is the bowl.

On the left side of the shirt, there are seventeen abstract, anthropomorphic figures. Each was drawn with a head and a torso, but only one leg. This is a typical convention used at that time to illustrate enemies killed.

It is clear that the warrior–artist is depicting the honors he has earned in battle. One can interpret the drawing to mean that the owner of this shirt has gone to battle many times; he was the pipe carrier on fourteen occasions, and has overcome seventeen enemies in battle.

Numakiki (Mandan)
Shirt, (back), about 1820
Opposite: back (detail)
Collection history: purchased by George G. Heye
in Paris, France, and accessioned by NMAI in 1929.
16.5277

55

This shirt was originally catalogued as Lakota or Dakota, but the exact tribal affiliation is unclear. The tribes in the upper Missouri River region traded in a vast network, so any of them could have created this shirt.

This shirt and the Mandan shirt 16.5277 (page 55) were probably created within the same time frame. The warrior–artists of both garments illustrated their exploits in a similar way, though the Mandan warrior–artist drew the pipes horizontally and the figures vertically, while the Lakota/Dakota warrior–artist drew both elements horizontally.

On both shirts, the warrior–artists used a familiar convention for depicting pipes: a wide horizontal bar with an inverted triangle at one end representing the pipe bowl. Also on both shirts, each figure was drawn as only a head, torso, and single leg.

At the same time, the drawings on the two shirts differ in certain ways. The Lakota/Dakota warrior–artist added red paint to his pipes and filled in the body of the figures. The red bodies could have been colored solely for aesthetic purposes, or their color could be a reference to a specific tribe. The series of red bands on some of the pipe bowls could represent different levels of authority, although this, too, is uncertain.

It is also unclear why the warrior–artist of this shirt chose to illustrate both the pipes and the figures horizontally. Most likely he decided that the horizontal orientation on both sides of the shirt created a balanced composition.

The style of quillwork on this shirt also differs from that of the Mandan shirt. The Mandan artist used a quilling technique called single-quill technique, where quills are arranged in small bands of color perpendicular to the orientation of the quilled strip. The Lakota/Dakota woman used a quilling technique called multi-quilled plaiting, in which quills are folded at an angle over one another. This gives the appearance of small, triangular shapes of color, enhancing the quillwork's beauty.

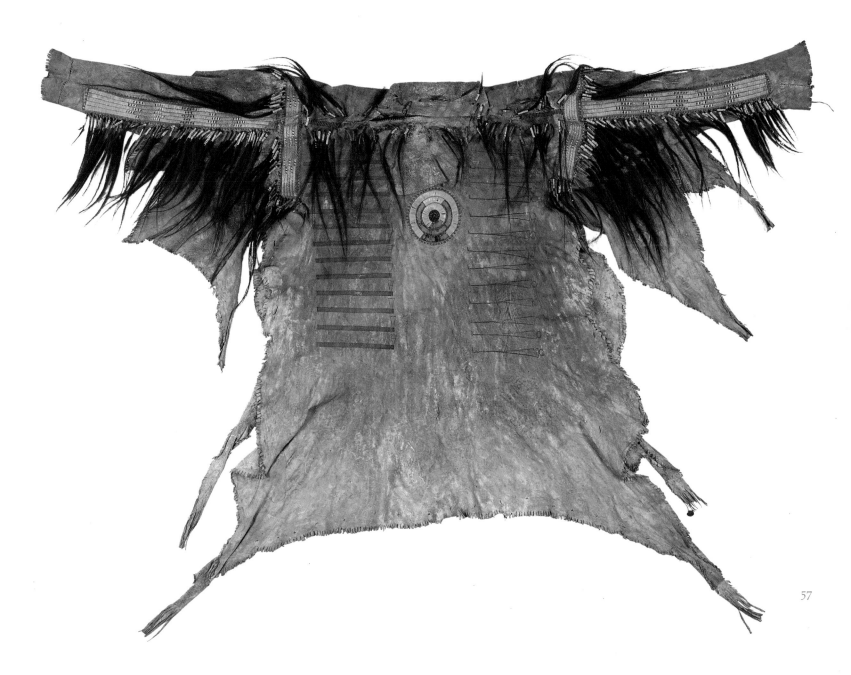

57

Upper Missouri
Shirt (back), about 1830
Opposite: back (detail)
Collection history: purchased by George G. Heye
00.7085

This shirt is catalogued as Blackfeet, but it could have been created by a member of any number of tribes located in the upper Missouri region in the early nineteenth century. This shirt is significant for several reasons. The warrior–artist added figurative details not commonly seen in pictographic drawings of the same time period. Also, the woman who created the quilled strips and beadwork had an exceptional command of her art.

The quill artist used multiple quills simultaneously, plaiting them onto the shirt's surface. This is an incredibly difficult technique, seldom used today. The technique allowed her to cover large areas of a surface with porcupine quills. The quills are somewhat woven and layered over one another. The quillwork is attached to the shirt on the edges. Using this technique, the artist could incorporate colored patterns into her work, taking advantage of the diamond-shaped designs that are formed when the quills are layered. On this shirt, she has chosen to use four colors—black, red, white, and light yellow. The primary color of the quilled strips is yellow, and in the center of each band is a series of designs. In the center, the artist put a cross design highlighted on the ends by a series of white-and-black diamond shapes. On the edges of the quilled areas, she applied a row of blue-and-white pony beads, two colors often seen on material from the early 1800s.

On both sides of this shirt, the warrior–artist depicted his battle exploits. On the front, he has drawn a horse, two figures, and battle accoutrements. Reading the story from right to left, we learn that the warrior–artist rode up to his enemy on a horse, which was outfitted for battle. Two eagle feathers are tied to the horse's tail and two to its mane—one in front and the other in the back. The warrior has also drawn an interesting detail radiating away from the horse's jaw: the four zigzag lines ending with black circles symbolize spiritual medicine that would help protect the horse in battle.

This horse wears a blanket with a saddle and stirrups. The warrior–artist indicated the saddle simply by showing saddle horns on the top of the horse. The rectangular shape that starts at the horse's back and hangs below its stomach is the saddle blanket. The artist has also drawn two stirrups. Instead of showing only one stirrup on each side of the horse, he drew two, side-by-side, hanging from the horse's stomach. This horse also wears a bridle.

A series of dashes starts from the bottom of the horse blanket and leads to a figure. These dashes represent the tracks of the shirt's owner, who has dismounted to engage the enemy. The warrior–artist has drawn the figures in a style commonly seen on shirts of the early 1800s. Long torsos and circular heads characterize the figures, and the only details shown are those associated with the warrior's military rank and battle accoutrements. This style of figure often has shaded arms and legs, but the torso is usually transparent, or slightly colored to indicate clothing. This

59

Upper Missouri
Shirt (front), about 1820
Overleaf: back (detail)
Collection history: purchased from W. O. Oldman,
London, England, accessioned by NMAI in 1910.
02.9035

figure wears a military society sash hanging from his right side. He wears an eagle feather in his hair, and holds a painted shield and a long lance, which he uses to overtake his enemy. Behind this figure are a bow and a rifle. The placement of these two weapons on the path of his approach indicates that he purposefully dropped them when he engaged in close combat. In many instances, a warrior was not obliged to kill the enemy; instead, he demonstrated his bravery in battle and gained honor by not using his weapons.

The warrior's enemy, shown on the left side of the shirt, holds a bow and arrow in each hand. He is Pawnee, illustrated by the figure's scalp-lock coiffure and high-topped moccasins. Between the enemy and the warrior is a Pawnee arrow that has missed the warrior.

The dashes, which reference the warrior–artist's footprints, begin between the Pawnee and the warrior–artist, lead past the Pawnee and around the side of the shirt, showing that the warrior continued in battle after the first encounter.

On the upper chest of the shirt are six vertical pipes with red pipe bowls, three on each side. Drawn next to the right quill band are seven anthropomorphic figures, shown with only torsos, heads, and hair. These figures symbolize Pawnee men the warrior–artist has defeated in battle. The pipes signify that he has led six battle expeditions against the enemy.

A similar scene appears on the back of the shirt. The mounted warrior–artist holds a quirt in one hand, and uses a United States flag as a lance in the other hand. The details in this self-portrait give us some valuable insight into the warrior's alliances. Under close examination, we see the warrior–artist has drawn a peace medal around his neck; the red symbolizes the ribbon and the yellow the color of the medal. The trail on the left goes around the horse to two heads, one with a Pawnee hairstyle. These probably symbolize enemies he defeated during the battle drawn on the lower half of the shirt. The other anthropomorphic figures pictured on the left side of the shirt near the quill strip symbolize enemies the warrior has defeated over time.

The horses on this shirt were painted with particular skill and style. The warrior–artist had apparently studied horses in order to portray the profile accurately. The horses have stylized legs and graceful necks, and are positioned to appear frozen in action. The eyes of each animal show that it is focused during battle, yet wild in spirit.

61

This extraordinary shirt is visually appealing and has an important collection history. According to NMAI records, Thomas S. Twiss collected this shirt about 1850. Although it is catalogued as Chiracahua Apache, this attribution is unlikely.

Thomas S. Twiss was born in 1803 in New York, N.Y., to a prominent family. He was trained at West Point Academy from 1882 to 1826, where he ranked second in his class. He served as an officer and professor at West Point until 1829, and later taught at South Carolina College, now the University of South Carolina.

In 1855, Major Twiss became the first European-American to be appointed an Indian agent to the upper Platte River region. When he first arrived at Ft. Laramie, Twiss was known to be harsh in his dealings with the Indian people. But his stance softened when he married Mary Standing Elk, a member of the Spleen Band of Oglala Lakota, later that year. The Oglala Lakota gave Standing Elk the name of Wanikiyewin, or Saves the Tribe, because

of her influence upon Twiss. Twiss was not present when the Ft. Laramie Treaties of 1851 and 1868 were signed, but his hand was evident.

The painting on this shirt is unusual. It is the most detailed example of abstract pictographic representation in this book. Four basic forms are represented on this shirt: shields, lances, fans, and war bonnets.

A row of five shields is evident on the shirt's front right side. The top three shields are adorned with eagle feathers around their perimeters. The feathers are shown here as long black lines that widen at the tips. Each of these three shields has a series of dots near the center, and a red band painted around the edge. The red band probably represents red wool cloth, which was an important trade commodity during that time period. The lower

63

Upper Missouri Region
Shirt (front), about 1858
Overleaf: back (detail)
Collection history: collected by Thomas S. Twiss, Indian agent at Ft. Laramie, Wyoming, from 1885 to 1861, and presented to NMAI by Harmon W. Hendricks. 08.8017

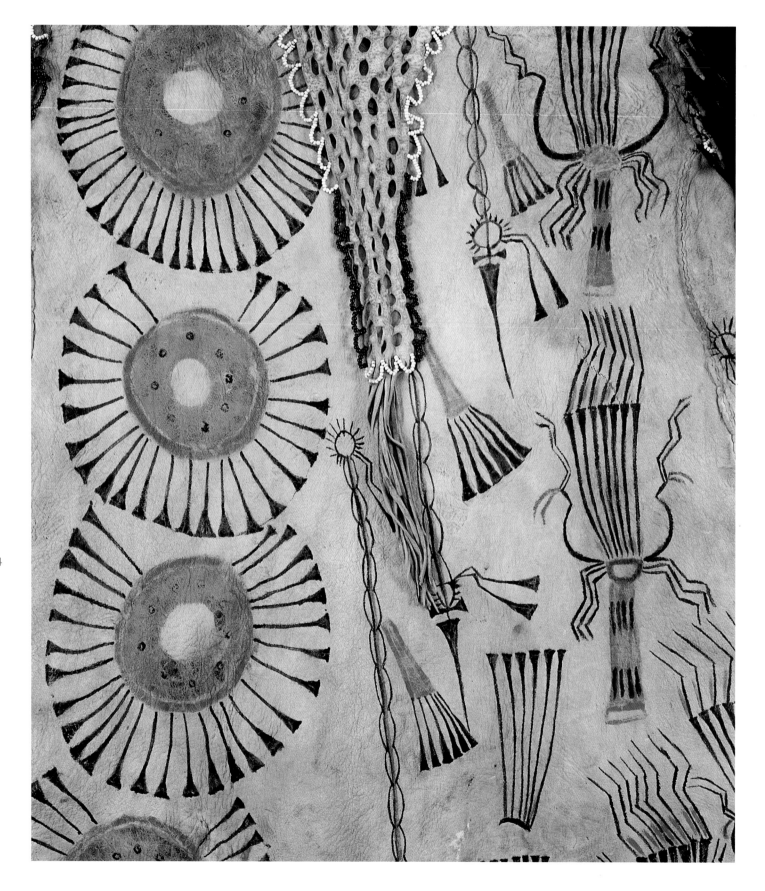

two shields are undecorated. On the left side of the shirt, one can see two lances and a war bonnet. A lance was an effective weapon for a mounted warrior. Lance images symbolize men's military societies. This lance was drawn vertically with the tip pointed down. The abstract feathers are attached horizontally to the lance shaft. The thick red line running parallel to the shaft represents red wool trade cloth. A feather extension has been added in the middle of the lance, probably for decoration.

To the left of the lance are two feathered, split-horn war bonnets. One has a long, feathered trailer, the other a short one, shown as irregular red rectangles below the green circles. A war bonnet is a sign of distinction. Like a decorated shirt, a war bonnet signifies that the wearer is an accomplished warrior and well respected among his people. Only someone held in the highest esteem would own a long, feathered-trailer war bonnet.

This warrior–artist illustrated these war bonnets unconventionally. The small green circle on the lower center of the war bonnet is the wearer's head. Eagle feathers stand vertically from the wearer's head, while long fringe, possibly ermine tails, radiates from each side. The zigzag lines that come from the tops of the feathers are probably decorative red feather tufts.

Similar scenes adorn the back of the shirt. On the right are four heads wearing feathered war bonnets, and four lances, probably indicating that the men wearing the war bonnets carried decorated lances. These lances are different from those on the front of the shirt. On these lances, a series of half circles runs along each shaft. These illustrate that the lance was wrapped in fur, a typical practice in the 1800s. A leather thong was wrapped around the fur, securing it to the shaft, and creating bulges of fur.

Below the lower lance are two groups of feathers attached to a horizontal line; these are feathered fans. On the left side of the shirt is a series of four decorated shields.

Two long, triangular neck facings hanging on the front and back of this shirt have been cut with a series of decorative holes. Among the many tribes of the Plains, especially the A'Aninin and Blackfeet, however, entire shirts were thus pierced. A good example is Blackfeet shirt 14.3567 (page 39) in the Shirts of Power section of this catalogue. Pierced shirts probably indicated spiritual power.

65

This beautifully constructed and painted shirt is unusual. There are few known examples of this particular figurative drawing style, making it difficult to attribute the craftsmanship to a specific tribal group. The garment was originally identified as "Mandan Sioux," which is misleading as the Mandan and the Lakota (Sioux) are two different tribes. A Crow buffalo hide painting in the collections of the National Museum of the American Indian bears a striking resemblance to the drawing style on this shirt.

The quilled strip, common to early robes, employs the quill-wrapped-horsehair technique, which indicates it was made between 1830 and 1840. Other examples of this technique are held in several European museums, including the Berne Historical Museum in Germany. These examples, too, feature figures wearing pointed devices on their heads. The similarities indicate that the same tribal group probably created all of them.

Author and cultural scholar Bill Holm, who has conducted extensive research on this style of drawing, believes the tribal affiliation of this shirt, and other similar examples, may be either Crow or Hidatsa. The artist or artists who drew on this shirt were well versed in the pictographic tradition and had developed a style that is both elegant and visually powerful.

There are a total of five battle scenes on this shirt, three on the back and two on the front. On the back, the three battle scenes are organized horizontally, one on top of the other. In the top row, the victor of this battle is shown on the right side near a shield bearing two dots, each with a zigzag pointing down. He moves from right to left, first overtaking the standing enemy holding a rifle, then using the captured rifle against a second, long-haired enemy on the left. The vertical line with five horizontal lines radiating from it to the right of the enemy with the tomahawk symbolizes the victor's hand. The warrior–artist is telling us that he took the enemy's tomahawk during battle.

The two horses in the center row are part of the next battle scene. The victor, mounted on the right, has taken a rifle away from the mounted enemy (who uses a saddle), shown by the hand symbol as in the previous scene. These gracefully rendered horses demonstrate the warrior–artist's skill as a draftsman and keen observer. He chose to include only the important elements of each horse, while preserving the essential beauty of the animal.

In the bottom row, the figure wearing a coat on the right side is the victor during this exchange. He is a well-respected man in his community, as we can see by his war bonnet and military frock coat. He uses his rifle against the enemy, who tries to use his bow. The shield next to this victor is the same shield that has been shown consistently on this side of the coat, evidence that the same warrior performed all of the exploits on this side of the shirt.

Upper Missouri Region
Shirt (front), about 1840
Overleaf back (detail)
Collection history: purchased by George G. Heye
in London, England, and accessioned by NMAI in 1930.
17.6345

The two scenes shown on the front of the shirt are like those on the back, but here the victor is shown on the left side of the shirt. He has the same shield used in the previous scenes. Interestingly, the warrior–artist's depiction of his enemies is slightly different on this side of the shirt. Here, they are shown with pointed headgear. It is unclear whether this signifies a hairstyle or is an artistic convention used to show that his enemy is from a certain tribal group or area. Three of his foes wear high-top moccasins, indicated by the flaring sides just below the shin. In other Plains Indian drawings, this detail signifies a figure is Pawnee. The artist portrays all his enemies wearing earrings, another Pawnee convention. Some of the figures carry powder horns, illustrated by the crescent-shaped designs near their hips.

A warrior on each side of this shirt wears a war bonnet. On the front, the war bonnet has a trailer. It is interesting to note how the warrior–artist chose to depict the feathers with the shaft shown as a thin line, ending in a triangular shape. There are few known examples of feathers depicted this way. The feathers on shirt 08.8017 (page 63) have been drawn in this fashion. Also, the graphic treatment of the heads in both examples is similar.

In this drawing, the Ute warrior-artist Yellow Nose has dismounted his horse, and, while holding its reins, counts coup against the enemy. Yellow Nose's drawing shows that the enemy was a well respected and accomplished warrior. He wears a war shirt decorated with beaded strips and fringe, and a horned bonnet associated with a military society in his tribe. Yellow Nose has also illustrated his enemy's weapons—a rifle and a staff. The warrior–artist included these items to show that his enemy was armed, and in overcoming him, Yellow Nose demonstrates his bravery.

When Yellow Nose was about four years old, the Arapaho and Cheyenne captured him and his mother. He was later adopted by the Cheyenne Chief Spotted Wolf, and became an accomplished warrior and artist. In keeping with tradition, he was raised in the culture of his adopted tribe (Maurer, 202).

Yellow Nose
Ute (raised as Cheyenne)
Drawing, about 1879–80
Collection history: collected in 1880–81 by Major John Gregory Bourke;
presented to NMAI by Anna Bourke Richardson, accessioned in 1964.
23.4252

Although this shirt is catalogued as having been collected by Thomas S. Twiss at Fort Laramie, Wyoming, in 1850, its style leaves this collection history in question. Important details such as hairstyle, shield designs, and some facial features are more closely associated with pictographic styles employed after 1850.

On the front of this shirt the Cheyenne warrior–artist has portrayed himself defeating two of his enemies. Both of these men are Crow, indicated by their pompadours and hair extenders, and the red paint on the top half of their faces. It was common practice for Crow warriors to wear hair extenders in battle. A series of hair locks was attached to a thong and tied to the head. Tree pitch would be added at spaced intervals to keep the sections together. The Crow shown on foot wears a hair extender. The long lines extending from the back of his head are the locks of hair, and the cross-hatching is the pitch that holds them together.

As in most pictographic scenes, the sequence of action moves from right to left. In the first scene on the right, the warrior–artist is shown mounted on his horse, carrying his shield, and wearing hair ornaments. His horse is prepared for battle, illustrated by the eagle feathers tied to its mane. His shield provides us insight to an aspect of his spiritual life. Traditionally, designs on shields are associated with visionary experiences. These experiences can come to the owner through ceremony or fasting or in a dream. Elements of the vision are drawn on a shield for protection during battle. The warrior transfers some of his spiritual energy by incorporating in his shield design elements of his visionary experience. Hence, it is not just the physical properties of the shield that protect the warrior from harm in battle; it is also the power of the images painted on the shield.

A large black bird flanked by black-and-red semicircles is depicted on this shield. The bird probably references the Thunderbird, a mythical creature associated with power in traditional Plains Indian belief.

The warrior–artist is chasing a Crow man who is on foot. The warrior holds a rifle in one hand and a bow in the other. He wears a powder horn, shown as an uncolored crescent shape near his stomach. The object floating above his head is probably a horse quirt, symbolizing that the warrior–artist has counted coup on his enemy. Counting coup, the highest battle honor that can be achieved, is a system of touching the enemy while engaged in conflict. This honor was most dangerous and difficult to achieve. In this instance, the warrior–artist rode up to the Crow and counted coup with the horse quirt, shown here by a long triangular-shaped decoration. The warrior–artist purposefully included the enemy's weapons in his picture as evidence that his exploit was dangerous.

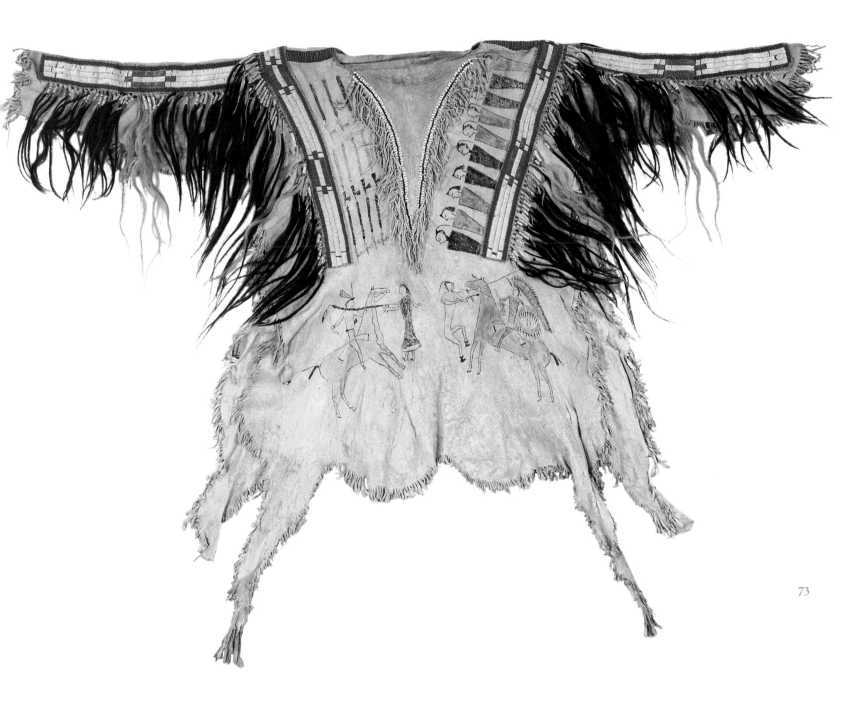

73

Tsethasetas (Cheyenne)
Shirt (back), about 1865
Overleaf: front (detail)
Collection history: presented to NMAI
by Harmon W. Hendricks and accessioned in 1918.
08.8034

In the next series of painted events, the warrior–artist has ridden up to the mounted Crow illustrated on the left side of the shirt. This Crow man also wears a powder horn and carries a rifle. Four lines radiating from the barrel of the rifle show that the warrior–artist was under fire during his brave deeds. Two long red rectangles projecting from the Crow's hips indicate his breechcloth. The white paint at the ends of his breechcloth is an important detail, because the trade wool that was commonly used at this time had such white edges.

A bow floating above the head of the mounted Crow indicates the warrior–artist counted coup against him. The arrow projecting below the right arm shows that after the warrior–artist counted coup, he shot the enemy with an arrow.

Two battle scenes appear on the back of this shirt. The mounted warrior on the right is probably not the owner of this shirt. We know this because he is wearing a full war bonnet with trailer, indicating high status in his community. He also holds a shield and rifle. This warrior, an ally of the warrior–artist, has ridden up to a Pawnee, shown with a typical Pawnee hairstyle and wearing black high-top Pawnee moccasins. A long lance near the horse's head aims towards the Pawnee, indicating that this ally used a lance against the enemy. In response, the Pawnee holds a bow and arrow, prepared to shoot at the mounted warrior.

The mounted warrior on the left side of the shirt is probably the warrior–artist who painted and wore this shirt. The main character on the front of the shirt is similar to this one. They both wear a topknot hairstyle, in which the hair is gathered above the forehead and wrapped tightly, allowing the wearer freedom of movement. Both also wear similar hair ornaments, a cross-hatched triangle tied to an eagle feather. Thus, we can assume they are both self-portraits.

The warrior–artist's yellow horse has been painted with a zigzag line starting from its head and ending in the middle of its front leg. This zigzag line symbolizes lightning and is meant to provide the horse with protection and power. The warrior holds a bow in one hand and a lance in the other. His quiver can be seen just above his hips, on the far side of his body. His lance is different from that of his comrade; it is thicker and has a series of bumps running its length. Lances were often wrapped with hide or fur, usually buffalo. When wrapped and tied, the shaft of the lance appears bumpy from a distance. In this scene, the warrior–artist is overtaking his enemy, who is a woman. Occasionally, women accompanied men on war parties and participated in battle.

Like another shirt in this catalogue, 02.9035 (page 59), this shirt shows the warrior–artist's battle prowess by recording the upper bodies of his defeated enemies in the upper chest region on both sides of the shirt. These figures were drawn in more detail than those on the other shirt. Here, the warrior–artist included facial features in profile, such as eyes, nose, and chin. He has also shown details that illustrate tribal affiliation. The Pawnee are shown with their distinctive hairstyle, and the Crow are shown with long hair and a pompadour.

The artist also records the number of war parties he has led by drawing pipes in the same area. His color selection for the pipes is important to note. Some of the pipes are shown more realistically, using a dark stem and a red pipe bowl, as red is the color of pipestone. He has also colored contrasting rows of pipes using the same color scheme, but reversed.

In this drawing, Red Dog has made a portrait of his friend, Few Tails, who wears a fringed war shirt. Red Dog paid particular attention to Few Tails's shirt, including the beaded chest and arm strips, and the arm fringe. The beading design on this shirt is similar to that of 00.9446, shown on page 149. Red Dog emphasized the extensions that hang from the bottom of Few Tails's shirt. War shirts are constructed using the hides of two animals, with the animals' legs hanging from the lower portion of the shirt, just as Red Dog has illustrated here.

Red Dog has also given us important information about Few Tails and his horse. He portrays his friend riding a large, strong, but graceful animal, shown by the positioning of the horse's legs and its raised head. The horse has been painted for battle, from its nose down the front legs, and from its rump down the rear legs. The painted wavy line refers to lightning, which, according to Plains lore, would empower and protect the horse in battle. We know that Few Tails's horse has been in battle before, because a scalp lock hangs from its mouth, evidence of its valor. Few Tails is portrayed with both arms extended as if to show us his shirt, and he holds a lance to use against his enemy.

Red Dog
Lakota (Sioux)
Portrait of Few Tails, about 1884
Collection history: collected by Dr. V. T. McGillycuddy, Indian Agent at Pine Ridge Indian Reservation, South Dakota; given to NMAI by Eleanor Sherman Fitch, and accessioned in 1943.
20.6230

Yellow Nose portrays High Wolf counting coup with his riding quirt against a Nez Perce. High Wolf wears a beaded or quilled war shirt into battle. Yellow Nose has included a glyph above High Wolf's body: a drawing of a wolf with long legs, referring to High Wolf's name. A line connects the glyph to High Wolf, making its meaning clear. Name glyphs were often included in pictographic drawings as a way to record whose deed is depicted.

High Wolf's tracks are shown as dashes that start at the middle of the horse and lead to the enemy, an important detail Yellow Nose included to aid in telling the story.

77

Yellow Nose
Ute (raised as Cheyenne)
Portrait of High Wolf, about 1879–80
Collection history: collected in 1880–81 by Major John Gregory Bourke,
presented by Anna Bourke Richardson, and accessioned by NMAI in 1964.
23.4368

This finely tailored coat has been decorated with short fringe along the edging, down the back, and around the neck and arms. It closes in the front with buttons, an idea probably inspired from European-American tailoring. This jacket is a good example of a garment that has incorporated Western tailoring, but is decorated with Plains Indian designs and embroidered in the traditional way with quills.

Figural quillwork is incredibly difficult to execute. Most quillwork is applied in a series of straight lines that curve slightly to conform to the shape of the object being decorated. But here the artist had to manipulate her quills in tight curves while varying the thickness of her line to conform to the design. There are many designs on this jacket, including figural heads and abstract geometrics.

On the lower portion of the jacket, we see a series of anthropomorphic heads, six in front and four in back. We know these figures symbolize men from the Crow tribe who were longtime enemies of the Lakota and Dakota. They wear Crow pompadour hairstyles and a band of red paint on their foreheads, a known Crow style of battle paint. As on other pictorial shirts, these images reference the owner's war record. We can read that the owner of this jacket defeated ten of his enemies in battle. On the front, four of the figures, two on each side, are shown with bleeding neck wounds suffered during battle. On the back, one of the figures wears an earring.

Running up the shirt's center and around the neck are repeating designs, each with three facing finger-like motifs topped by elongated ovals. There are several possible interpretations for these. Many Dakota designs are either geometric, illustrating Plains influence, or floral, reflective of Great Lakes/Woodlands influence. These designs could be floral, with the finger-like motifs representing the leaves of a plant, and the oval representing the flower. Feather patterns radiate from each of the flowers, probably representing petals. But around the neck, the artist quilled a series of opposing leaves and chose not to illustrate the flower with petals.

Another interpretation of this design is that the finger-like motifs represent the spider, a powerful symbol among the Lakota, who are the Dakota's closest relatives. According to

Dakota

Shirt (front), about 1880

Opposite: back; overleaf: front (detail)

Collection history: purchased by George G. Heye,
accessioned by NMAI in 1913.

03.2912

traditional Lakota stories, the spider, known as Iktomi, has many powers including the power of protection. The spider is associated with Double Woman, a supernatural being commonly thought to have originated the art of porcupine-quill decoration. According to anthropologists who have studied the Lakota, women who belong to the Double Woman society conduct a secret ceremony in which a child "is taken out to a lonely place. There the women make a swing or hammock-like structure in the form of the spider-web design, supported at each of its four corners. The child is placed upon it. This is intended to bring good fortune to the child. A design of the spider-web might then be placed upon the robe of the child as a symbol of its having experienced the ceremony" (Wissler, 50).

The spider design on this garment would also protect its wearer. According traditional Lakota beliefs, a spider-web cannot be destroyed by bullets or arrows (since they pass through it). Within the context of this jacket, which also illustrates the battle exploits of its owner, the spider-web design tells the story of the shirt's owner. Perhaps he used the protective powers of Iktomi in battle, or perhaps he experienced the Double Woman ceremony as a child. The pictures indicate he defeated many Crow enemies, and counted coup upon the enemy using his bow, which has been quilled on the back of his jacket.

81

Drawings that illustrate warrior–artists' battle deeds are most commonly found on shirts and robes and in ledgers and sketchbooks. A large robe provided the warrior–artist with a greater drawing surface than a much smaller shirt. Thus, the robe allowed him to tell the stories of his accomplishments in greater detail, whereas a shirt allowed only enough space to give a basic narrative of the battle. In either case, a warrior–artist told his version of a story. Although the names of many artists have been lost, their work remains a statement of personal achievement and artistic style.

This robe, painted by His Horse Looking, illustrates his participation in battles against the Crow, Pawnee, and U.S. government soldiers. He painted in the classic Plains Indian style of the late nineteenth century, using artistic conventions to show the battle's action. For instance, a flash from a gun and a series of hoof prints on the lower center of the hide illustrate that enemies were mounted and shooting guns at the Lakota. (See detail on the next page.)

His Horse Looking
Lakota (Sioux)
Robe, about 1885
Overleaf: detail
Collection history: collected by F. M. Covert from Lakota Chief His Horse Looking,
at Rapid City, South Dakota; accessioned by NMAI in 1904.
00.1029

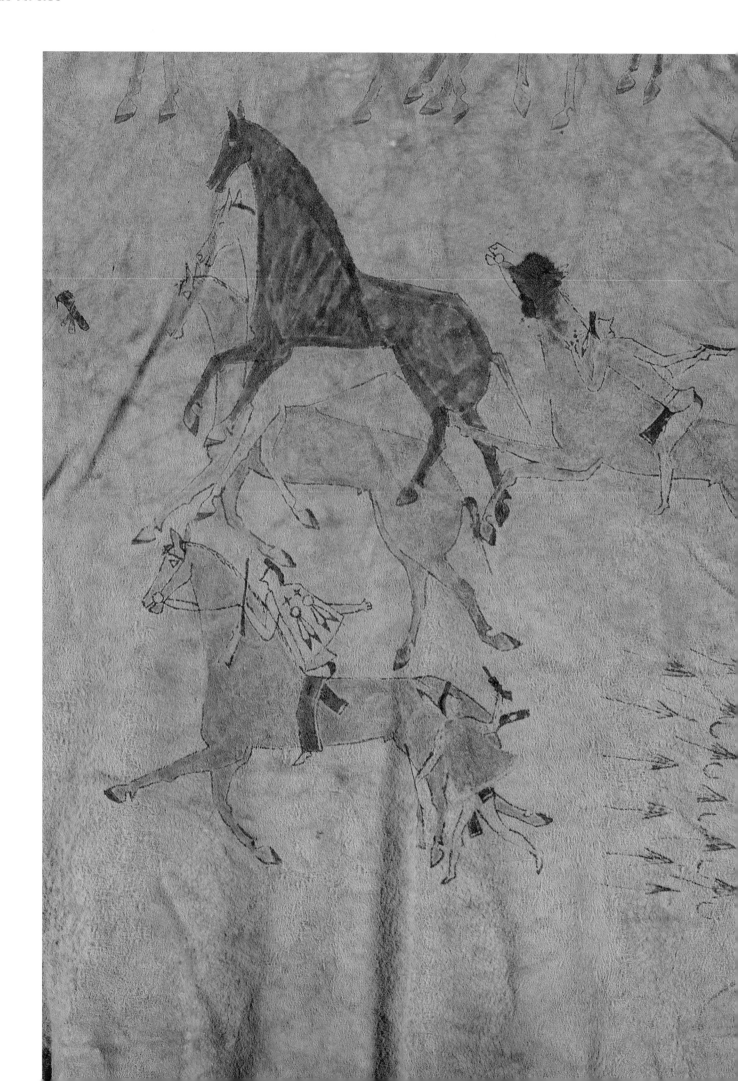

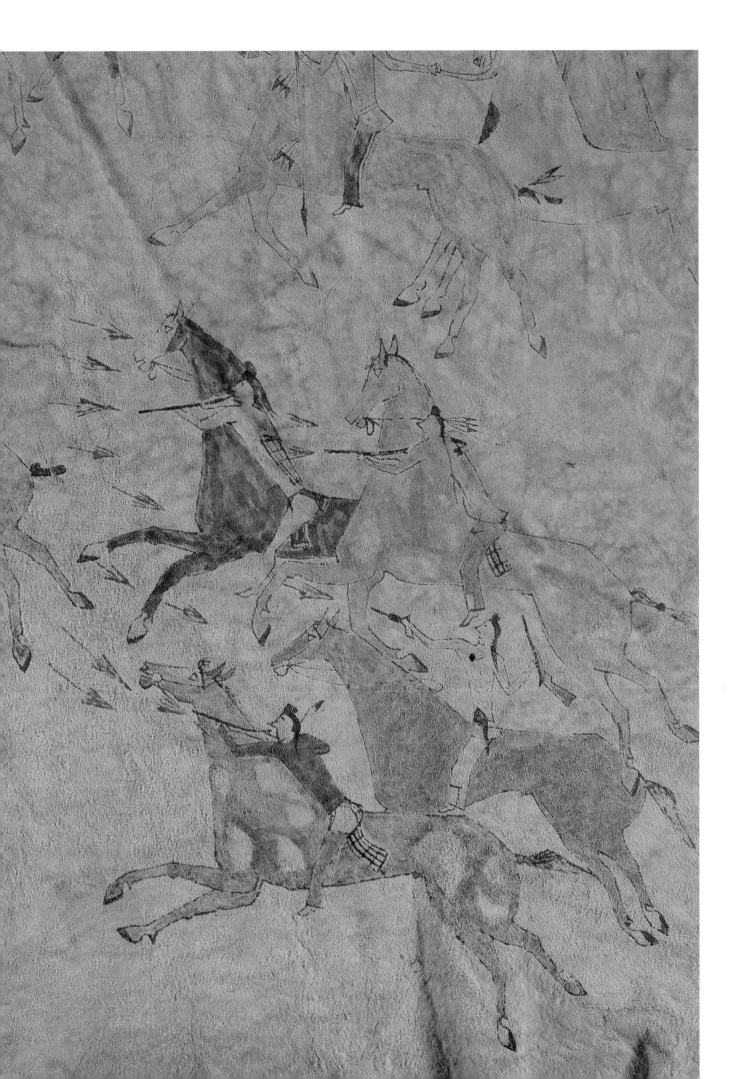

"We're still struggling today as Native Americans. . . . And we're trying to maintain sovereignty. . . . And we're still trying to take our place in that structured society in a good way by maintaining the uniqueness that we have as people. That's what God has given to us."

PAULINE SMALL (APSAALOOKE)

EACH AMERICAN INDIAN TRIBE is special in its own way. The Crow or Apsaalooke (Children of the Long Beaked Bird) people are particularly distinctive. Separating from the Hidatsa people in North Dakota more than 250 years ago, the Crow moved west and south until they settled in the Yellowstone River valley in south central Montana, where they now reside on the Crow Indian Reservation.

Over the years, historical forces have obliged the tribe to adapt—physically, mentally, militarily, and aesthetically—in order to survive. In those early roaming days, which play a large part in Crow legend and oral history, the beauty and richness of Crow life drew the attention, and sometimes envy, of other tribes. As a result, constant inter-tribal altercations took place. Seeking allies, the Crow people befriended white newcomers when they arrived in the early 1800s. But constant military pressure continued to come from the Lakota to the east, the Blackfeet to the northwest, and, on occasion, the A'aninin and Cree to the north.

Despite this turbulence, the Crow people's tribal traditions not only survived but thrived. Warriors developed into great leaders and traders, and the people became strong and confident—even boastful. Perhaps because of the abundance of natural resources available to them, including bighorn sheep, bear, buffalo, otter, ermine, beaver, deer, and eagles, Crow artists encountered few restrictions as they fashioned creations unequaled anywhere on the Plains.

Students of Plains Indian art well appreciate the beauty of Crow artwork as traditionally expressed in painted rawhide items, baby carriers, otter-fur quivers, gun cases, horse trappings, robes, moccasins, beadwork, and quillwork. But the Crow are most highly renowned for their distinctive use of color and their exquisite shirts. Many Crow artistic skills have stood the test of time and can be seen at the annual Crow Fair on the reservation in August.

The high quality of materials, aesthetics, and workmanship renders traditional artwork made by the Crow (Apsaalooke) people among the best of all Plains Indian art. The wide, pastel-colored beaded strips highlighted by triangles and hourglass shapes and framed by contrasting borders immediately identify this tribal style.

The long, white fur fringes tipped with black are from the ermine, more commonly known as the weasel. This animal lives in the northern regions of North America. In summer, its coat is brown and it is called a weasel. In winter, its fur turns white and luxurious, and the weasel becomes known as the ermine.

The Plains Indian people sometimes attached the entire ermine fur pelt to their clothing for decoration. A more common practice was to trim a section of the pelt's back, to where the tail connects, and sew the back skin into a tube, making an extra long "tail." On occasion, artists would substitute white rabbit fur for ermine, with skunk fur providing the black tip.

White ermine fur with its contrasting black tip added beauty to the garment and the artist hoped some of the animal's fierceness would be transferred to the wearer.

Apsaalooke (Crow)
Shirt (back), about 1880
Collection history: collected by W. Wildschut
about 1920, accessioned by NMAI in 1924.
13.5991

Plains Indian shirts all have stories to tell. In addition to its aesthetic beauty (similar to shirt number 01.1110 pictured on page 35), this quill-wrapped-horsehair shirt also chronicles the dynamic commerce among tribes on the northern Plains.

Many people today believe that early Indians supplied all of their own needs from the land. Like many other ideas about American Indians, this simply is not true. All people have needs that they are unable to satisfy, and all cultures have bartered with others for desired goods. Most of North America's northern Plains have, at one time or another, been home to Native people. This geographical area provided abundant raw materials, such as buffalo hide and meat, berries and corn, which could be processed into trade goods, such as tanned robes, moccasins and clothing. Residents could trade those items for goods they required, such as seashells, and later, horses, blankets, and guns.

Before the arrival of the Europeans, Native American trade routes and trade centers developed across the Plains, providing forums for exchange. In what is now the Washington/Oregon area, the Dalles Rendezvous on the Columbia River was well known as an important trade center for people from the Pacific and Plateau regions. In the northern Plains area most tribes traded at the Mandan/Hidatsa center, on the Missouri River in central North Dakota, and the Arikara Center, downriver (Taylor, 1984). The Shoshone Rendezvous in southwestern Wyoming was situated midway between coastal and Plains trading sites. So, an item made by the Cree people near the Great Lakes in Canada could conceivably have been brought to the North Dakota trading center and traded to the Crow people, who then might have taken it to the Shoshone Rendezvous in Wyoming to trade with the Nez Perce, who, in turn, could have traded it to the Chinook at the Dalles Rendezvous near the Pacific Ocean. We can now trace a vast network of exchange.

Tribes went to great efforts to make their materials suitable for trading and develop partners in commerce. Because of the great abundance of fur-bearing animals on the Plains, the creative Crow people became successful traders specializing in tanned buffalo robes and deerskin clothing. This early shirt may have been produced for trade.

93

Apsaalooke (Crow)
Shirt (back), about 1860
Collection history: Mrs. Edwin C. Ward
collection, accessioned by NMAI in 1922.
11.4243

Although this shirt or vest is catalogued as having been made by Blackfeet, Crow elders believe their tribe probably made it. These elders feel that it may have been made to be worn during parades and celebrations. As on other shirts, a beaded amulet has been attached to this vest, probably to impart spiritual power to the garment's owner.

94

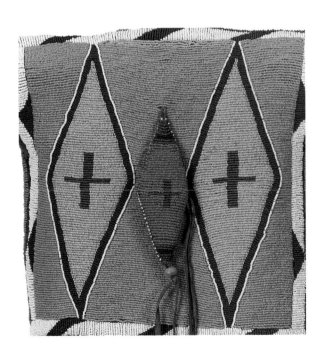

95

Apsaalooke (Crow)
Vest (front and back detail), about 1875
Collection history: purchased
and accessioned by NMAI in 1938.
19.7993

"The old timers used to go out and fast and sleep on cliffs. They had to have that spiritual belief that they might come out of the war unhurt."

TEDDY WILLIAMSON (PIKUNI)

AN IMPORTANT PART of the Plains area, southern Plains are home to people who developed their own art style. This region was settled primarily by tribes removed from their original homelands and each tribe brought its own aesthetic. These styles influenced one another to create a combination style. Although some tribes' artistic presentations are unique to them, such as the arts of the Osage, their decorative techniques can be recognized as originating in the southern Plains.

Instead of heavily decorating their materials with quills or beads, southern Plains artists followed the minimalist philosophy that less is more.

Southern Plains painting traditions are distinguishable by soft hues on moccasins, leggings, and other items, giving them a warm, conservative coloring that is very different from the white-tanned deerskin of northern Plains people. Southern Plains beadwork is also minimal, being used only as trim on many items of apparel. Southern Plains artists developed an easily recognizable, twisted-fringe technique that became another of their hallmarks. These variations, decorative motifs, and techniques create interesting contrasts to the artwork of their brethren to the north and elsewhere, and mark the southern Plains people as highly sophisticated artists.

98

Inunaina (Arapaho)
Shirt (front) about 1885
Collection history: collected by Dr. W. C. Barnard in Oklahoma,
and accessioned by NMAI in 1920.
10.3140

Inunaina (Arapaho)
Shirt (front), about 1885
Collection history: exchanged from James Economos,
and accessioned by NMAI in 1972.
24.7456

"I would have to say there was a purpose behind all of this. This is a purpose. And they always went out seeking all the time for some power that they may gain for their war purposes. I don't think that our people would be very strong without that spiritual background. And I think today people are still looking for that. They are still trying to find some spiritual [aspect] of their life to be led by."

EARL OLD PERSON (PIKUNI)

AS A PEOPLE TRAVEL life's pathway, fraught with the unknown, they often need to call for help. Some seek a four-leaf clover, while others may wish upon a falling star, or ask The One Above for help. Plains Indians, living in their vast world, are no exception.

In the early days the world was filled with mystery and wonder. Scientific understandings of such things as disease, death, the stars, the sun, wind, rain, lightning and other natural phenomena were unknown, and thus cried out for explanation. Within the various Indian cultures, stories from the ancestors addressed many of these mysteries, and dreams and visionary experiences explained others.

According to these stories, at one time our relatives, the animals, had the ability to speak with us. Their relationships with people were both positive and negative. For instance, many tribal groups tell stories about how Coyote created the world, but he is also sometimes shrewd and even cruel.

Traditional tribal stories tell of the loyalty of Dog, the strength of Bear, and the wisdom of Owl. Later, although we lost the ability to hear the animals, the creatures themselves never lost their power. Plains Indian people maintain a close ancient connection with these animals and their special gifts, and we continue to represent them in art. Most tribes use the feathers of the mighty eagle or hawk to evoke their strength, beauty, and hunting ability. Others make quivers from the otter for its beauty, or the cougar, to enlist its hunting skills. Clans and societies use the names of Wolves, Bears, and Dragonfly, which can fly so fast it seems to disappear.

Mothers hope to obtain special animal strengths for their children by fashioning amulets for the baby's navel in the shape of Turtle, who lives a long time, or Lizard, who is quick and can regenerate a part of its body.

This time-tested relationship between animal power and human wishes is still in force today. We gain strength from the bridges between animals and ourselves, evident in our family names, place names, and other reminders all around us.

This shirt is a classic example of the southern Plains style of decoration. Its simple, elegant lines and long, thin fringe give it an aesthetic power. An eagle's foot hangs from the bib on the front of the shirt, and a tail from a mule deer hangs from the bib on the back. All four legs of the deer hide, which hang from the lower portion of the shirt, have been decorated with carved deer dewclaws, which made an attractive clacking sound when the wearer moved.

Like many southern Plains shirts, this shirt is not heavily ornamented. Instead, its beauty lies in its simple design elements. For example, the shoulder portion is large, narrowing at the mid-section of the body, then flaring out again below the waist, giving it a graceful, contoured shape.

Two important animals are referenced on this shirt—the eagle and the mule deer. The eagle is revered by many tribes across the Plains, and the Cheyenne are no exception. According to traditional Cheyenne beliefs, the eagle possesses great protective power. Most Cheyenne men made their war bonnets with eagle feathers both to acquire protective powers and to show appreciation for the feathers' great beauty. The creator of this shirt has attached an eagle foot to it in hopes of transferring some of the eagle's protective power to the wearer.

The mule deer tail attached to this shirt also evokes power. Traditional Cheyenne people believe the mule deer is a great spiritual helper, with the ability to help or harm humans. A holy man is allowed to use this tail in ceremonies (Grinnell II, 104).

103

Tsethasetas (Southern Cheyenne)
Shirt (back), about mid-19th century
Collection history: from the S. K. Lothrop
collection and accessioned by NMAI in 1927.
15.3579

White Bull, also known as Ice, was a distinguished Cheyenne holy man. One of the four Old Man Chiefs of the Northern Cheyenne, he was probably the owner of this shirt, based on museum records. According to Cheyenne tradition, only a warrior who had counted coup in battle, and who was among the first to advance and the last to retreat during battle was allowed to wear a scalp shirt. If he were subsequently to fail to live up to these requirements, his shirt could be taken from him. He was expected to maintain high moral character, control his anger, and be calm even if bad luck were to strike his family.

Making a scalp shirt was considered a sacred act. When one shirt owner agreed to make a shirt for another man, noted warriors within the tribe gathered to pray and recount their war deeds, represented by each scalp lock attached to the shirt. A highly skilled woman who had been given the gift of quilling created the quillwork for the shirt (Powell, 46).

On this shirt, buffalo tracks have been quilled on the shoulder strips, perhaps referencing an animal spirit helper. On the lower portion of the shirt, a series of horse tracks has been drawn with three X's below. This may indicate that White Bull was in battle against many mounted enemies, and that during the battle he overcame three of them.

Tsethasetas (Northern Cheyenne)
Shirt (back) about 1855–1865
Opposite: detail
Collection history: collected from White Bull
at Upper (Northern) Cheyenne Agency,
Stephen Jewett collection, accessioned by NMAI in 1907.
01.3931

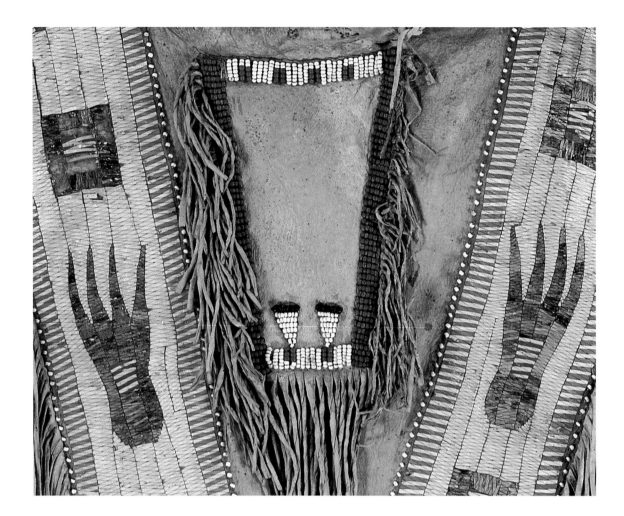

Among the Mandan, bears were thought to hold both spiritual and warrior powers that could be transferred to men through a visionary experience or in an actual physical encounter with the animal. The owner of this shirt, which features long quilled bear tracks on the chest, probably possessed bear power. Wearing the shirt honored his spiritual gift.

The quillwork on the strips is of the highest quality, further emphasizing the importance of the shirt and its wearer.

Obtaining power from bears is a consistent theme among many Plains Indian tribes. One of the earliest examples of the bear theme can be found among the petroglyphs at Castle Gardens in central Wyoming, which date from about 1625 to 1775. A series of bear tracks has been incised on the chest of a carved figure there, implying that the subject has acquired power from a bear, much like the owner of this shirt (Maurer, 25).

Imagine someone wearing this shirt as he rides a galloping horse—the long, swaying fringe adding visual power that is mindful of a mighty, charging bear.

107

Numakiki (Mandan)
Shirt (back), about mid-19th century
Opposite: detail
Collection history: collected at Fort Berthold
Indian Reservation, and bequeathed by De Cost Smith.
Accessioned into the NMAI collection in 1939.
20.1473

Although listed in museum's records as being of Jicarilla Apache origin, this shirt may be Ute. The Ute have a strong pony-bead tradition that lasted into the 1860s. They were also more likely than Jicarilla Apache to incorporate a European-style cut into their shirt design. The Ute were known to incorporate the Crow stitch or modified lazy stitch, as on this shirt, while the Jicarilla Apache used the lazy stitch.

In either case, the abstract beaded design probably represents a bear, a reference to the exploits of the shirt wearer, who may have killed a bear.

Indé (Jicarilla Apache)
Shirt (back), mid 19th century
Collection history: donated by Louis Boury
and accessioned by NMAI in 1923.
12.3380

During the nineteenth century, the Comanche occupied the southern Plains from western Oklahoma across Texas and into New Mexico. This child's parka is characteristic of Comanche clothing. It is made of lynx hide, sewn with the hair on the inside to keep the child warm, and constructed to use the lynx's tail, legs, and head. The hood of this parka is fashioned from the head of the animal. When a child wears the hood, the lynx's eyes and ears are clearly visible. The lynx's two front legs are used as sleeves, and its rear legs hang from the lower portion of the parka.

The lynx is a carnivorous animal that skillfully eludes other predators in the wild. Its elusive nature is said to be transferred to the child wearing this parka, ensuring that the wearer will be safe from harm and danger.

Niuam (Comanche)
Child's parka, about 1875
Collection history: collected by Mark Raymond Harrington
and accessioned into the NMAI collection in 1910.
02.1503

"These shirts, they're sacred to the people. And if they're to be given to anyone, they don't just give a shirt to somebody. There is going to have to be a transfer ceremony for one to take it. And it's not kept by one person all the time. After that person [who owned the shirt] has deceased, it's handed down, it's transferred to different people. And today, it's still going."

JOE OLD CHIEF (PIKUNI)

THE EIGHTEENTH AND NINETEENTH centuries brought waves of European-American settlers to the Plains, and with them devastating changes to traditional Plains Indian life, which had been fundamentally based on freedom. Reservations, boarding schools, and prisons forced and reinforced assimilation. Many of the changes that followed were tremendously destructive. Unfamiliar European diseases proved fatal to terrible numbers of Indians. The imposition of Christianity was one form of cultural oppression. Taking children from their homes and sending them to U.S. government-run boarding schools was another. Tribes that had been migratory were forced to stay in one place and attempt to live by farming. U.S. military actions and tribal conflicts were exacerbated by the forced relocation of tribes. Thus Native populations were ravaged and traditions suppressed.

Other meldings of European-American and Native American cultures may have been more benign, but they had far-reaching consequences nonetheless. As the Industrial Revolution reached the Plains, it brought with it new trade products that would change traditional Indian artwork forever. Beadwork using glass trade beads nearly replaced traditional quillwork. Shirts, once stitched from animal hides, were now made from wool and cotton and fitted with quilled or beaded strips, or replaced altogether by factory-made clothing. American flags, floral patterns from European fabrics, and Christian crosses were incorporated into decoration. Festive clothing acquired new embellishments such as shell casings and coins. The Plains Indian shirt found new life when it was revamped by the master ribbonworkers of Oklahoma; their influence is seen in the geometric and abstract floral ribbon overlays of ribbon shirts today. Plains Indians have reinterpreted their traditional styles—and their lives—many times over.

In 1972, after years of study, Alonzo Spang, a Northern Cheyenne Indian from Lame Deer, Montana, earned a Doctor of Education degree from Arizona State University. In honor of this great achievement, in the tradition of his forefathers, his family and friends presented him with a war shirt and leggings. In his words:

I ... spoke Cheyenne before I spoke English, and I used to interpret for my grandparents [the Limberhands], and they lived right next door. [My grandmother] ... didn't want me to go to college. She said, "You are going to become a white man, you are going to forget us." She said, "This is where you belong."

When I first graduated from high school, my goal was to get a degree in biological sciences. And biological sciences are as non-people-oriented as you can get. [When] you contrast it with education, it's just the opposite.

So I ... started college ... and then I transferred from there to the University of Montana (finally earning my M.A. in 1962 and the Ph.D. ten years later, both in Guidance and Counseling—both people skills). But later [my grandmother's] fears were alleviated or allayed because I didn't become a white man and still talked Cheyenne and still visited with her and spent time with her....

I think between my mom, you know, ... the two began ... [to talk with] the Kit Fox Society [about giving me this honor].... They gave their blessings and then ... it went on from there.

It took them ... about two years to gather ... enough buckskin to put the shirt together, and then the trousers and then the moccasins. The buckskin was tanned by my parents, and they always used a traditional Cheyenne tanning method....

See, I am named after Big Beaver. He was a warrior, and [the patterns in the shirt's beadwork] reflect his [symbols]. And I remember he performed the old traditional naming ceremony and I remember he painted me all red. This is a real significant color. [My female relative were the ones who did the beadwork.]

...The ceremony was held ... [in] a quonset building [behind the annex of the old tribal office building]. John Woodenlegs was president then ... and he was the main speaker and ... made the main presentation and, of course, [there] was a big celebration dance and feast.

[When I dance wearing this shirt, I am] very thankful that I am a Cheyenne and that I have been entrusted with some history. And it is an honor to put my outfit on and dance.

Tsethasetas (Northern Cheyenne)
Dr. Alonzo Spang's shirt (front), 1972
Opposite: back

This Western-style, tailored coat belonged to the Pawnee Lone Wolf, whose name has been beaded on the back. It combines European-American tailoring with traditional Plains Indian iconography. The tailoring includes a collar, a straight body, and an even-edged bottom hem, unlike traditional war shirts, which have no collars and often retain the animal legs at the bottom.

Although Plains Indian people have used the materials found in this shirt for decades, many of its designs show the influence of the white world. The lower hem of this jacket and the arms are decorated with five-pointed stars, which are rarely found on early Plains Indian garments. Christian-style crosses have been beaded onto the arms. Traditional Plains Indian elements on this jacket include beaded feathers around the neck, the designs on the arm strips and lower edges, hair locks on the arms, and a series of beaded dragonfly designs on the front. Dragonfly designs are found on many objects, including shields, moccasins, garments, and hair ornaments. Dragonflies symbolize strength, agility, and speed. A dragonfly darts quickly back and forth and is considered a predator of the insect world. Warriors used dragonfly designs hoping to gain such attributes.

117

Chaticks Si Chaticks (Pawnee)
Coat (front), about 1910
Opposite: back
Collection history: collected in Oklahoma by William M. Fitzhugh,
and accessioned into the NMAI collection in 1936.
19.3199

Deborah Magee Sherer, a contemporary Blackfeet artist, created this Bear Dreams Warshirt in 1977. Here she talks about her artwork:

> I had been "brainwashed" by white culture into thinking that the only "real" art was the "fine art" I had studied in college, which included painting, sculpture, printmaking, et cetera. Sure, I had grown up on the reservation seeing beadwork and dance outfits all of the time, but the really old, traditional ways of doing craftwork had been largely forgotten....
>
> Still, it took me a while to finally wake up and see what has been right under my nose all my life.... Thus, Bear Dreams Warshirt was the beginning of a deeply felt, deeply personal spiritual awakening. It took me four years to complete it.... I knew I had to dedicate it to the bear, which was appearing in many of my dreams.... This shirt [is] a personal expression, and should never be used for ceremonies.
>
> Now, when I attend Indian art shows, it is so inspiring to see artists going in new directions with traditional art forms. Our ancestors built a strong, lasting foundation for us, and I feel I'm standing on the shoulders of giants when I create a war shirt, a pipe bag, or a traditional bonnet.

Deborah Magee Sherer (Na-too-aki, or Sacred Woman)
Pikuni (Blackfeet)
Bear Dreams Warshirt (front), ©1977

The artist of this beautifully quilled coat incorporated many Western elements in her work. On the sleeves of this coat, she quilled stars and chevrons that must have been inspired by a United States military uniform showing rank. This type of decoration is, of course, not found on traditional Plains Indian shirts. The two eagles on the back of the coat, too, appear to have been inspired by a U.S. government icon. Alongside these adaptations, the artist maintained some traditional elements, including stepped triangles and crosses.

Indian people have used the American flag motif in their artwork for well over a hundred years. Considering U.S. mistreatment of Indians over the years, this choice seems antithetical. However, viewed from another perspective, it makes sense.

First, the flag is attractive: its colors, stripes, and stars make a pleasing configuration and a vivid aesthetic declaration. Perhaps more important, the flag represents not only the American political system and values, but also the physical place—the land the American Indian people have lived on for tens of thousands of years. It represents the sacred sites where we received gifts, such as tobacco, pipes, and corn. It represents our visions. It represents battlegrounds where we engaged invaders and where many died. And it also represents the sanctuary of our ancestors' remains and the land that will hold our bones as well.

This strong feeling for the U.S. flag can best be seen in Indian country and in our traditions. It is expected that when a young man graduates from high school he will volunteer for U.S. military service to perform his duty as a warrior. Upon returning home, Indian veterans are given many honors and privileges. At powwows only U.S. military veterans may carry the flag. At some celebrations, all the veterans dance together, filling the arena. So, while the flag conjures for some Americans a misty memory of "mom's apple pie," for us it's more aptly reminiscent of "grandma's dry meat."

Dakota (Eastern Sioux)
Coat (front), about 1890
Opposite: back
Collection history: from the John Jay White
collection, accessioned by NMAI in 1924.
10.4309

121

Remarkably, this shirt incorporates the brass fringe from the epaulets of a U.S. Army dress uniform, encircling quilled rosettes. Although we cannot speculate on how her people obtained this braided material, the artist's ingenuity is amply demonstrated. Plains artists are known for using materials creatively. In other pieces, artists used metal spoons as bells on horse equipment, coins as decorations on dresses and purses, buttons as decorations, and reshaped tin snuff can lids as jingle ornaments. At this late date it cannot be determined if the elaborate braided brass bullion was obtained in trade specifically to ornament a shirt, or whether it was won in battle and worn as a trophy. Both scenarios are plausible.

The basic orientation and painted style of this shirt identify it as having been made by the Lakota people, although the accession record states that it was collected from a man named Deaf Bear, a chief of the Crow Indian people in 1890.

The elegant, flowing, unencumbered freedom of this shirt is enhanced by its long leg-hide pendants and the cascading locks of hair.

Lakota (Sioux)
Shirt (front), about 1860
Collection history: collected by western artist Edwin Willard Deming
about 1893, and accessioned by NMAI in 1906.
00.9963

This wool ribbon shirt tells a story not in traditional painted pictographs, but in an abstract glass bead design. The beads are sewn on using the appliqué contour method, with the larger areas following the shape of the design element. Silk ribbons are sewn around the bottom of the shirt.

Only the maker and wearer of this shirt know the exact meaning of the design elements and colors, but we can speculate. The thunderbirds or eagles on the sleeves and the lower torso could set a spiritual foundation for the design. Both of these birds are sacred to the Plains Indian people. The front side shows the eagles connected to the American flag denoting that they are American. A male figure appears to be as brave and strong as a bear.

The figures on the back are accompanied by intriguing elements as well. The man is accomplished and wealthy because he owns more than one horse. Still, the figures maintain a physical attachment to their traditional past in their reliance upon the power of a bear. The scene takes place under a night sky filled with celestial bodies, with the hands controlling and blessing his world. The buffalo is the keystone of this world.

Jiwere (Oto)
Shirt (front) about 1900
Opposite: back
Collection history: collected by Mark Raymond Harrington
in Oklahoma, and accessioned by NMAI in 1923.
12.0838

This shirt, made of stroud wool trade cloth and fringed with buckskin, may have been used during the Tobacco Ceremony, which is one of the Crow people's oldest and most sacred ceremonies. For this ceremony, the Crow used short tobacco, not the type used for smoking. According to tribal lore, this protective tobacco was given to the Crow people by the stars. Through a series of ceremonies, the plant was grown and harvested. Successful harvests assured a family protection and good luck.

Early-nineteenth-century clothing used for the Tobacco Ceremony would certainly have been made of buckskin, but this shirt incorporates trade cloth that later became easily available. The small brass discs on the left side of the shirt may refer to stars, and the bundle tied on the right side of the shirt may contain sacred substances that would protect the wearer.

This small shirt was probably made for a child. During the latter half of the nineteenth century, children were allowed to be initiated into the Tobacco Society.

Apsaalooke (Crow)

Shirt (front), about 1915

Collection history: collected by William Wildschut at Crow Indian Reservation, Montana, in 1926, and accessioned into the NMAI collection in February 1929.

15.2395

127

This unusual garment—so long, it almost transcends the shirt classification into the cloak category—is thought to be somewhat experimental. The front opens from the neck to the bottom unlike a traditional poncho. Indeed, it is so unusual, we cannot say whether it was made within a cultural context or if it was a designer's trial that did not quite succeed.

The construction reveals the recycling practices of Plains Indian artists. The fantastically decorated shirt strips have been taken from a shirt dating to an earlier time. Such decorations are seen in European paintings of Indians made in the 1830s along the upper Missouri River. This remarkable quillworking technique goes beyond just wrapping and folding a quill between two parallel sewn threads. Here, small bundles of horsehair were wrapped in quills which were then sewn to the strip.

A shirt's decorative medium—quills or beads—was almost always applied to a strip of tanned animal hide rather than directly attached to the garment. The strip was then stitched to the shirt. Working this way was easier for the shirtmaker to handle. Furthermore, if the shirt became unwearable for any reason, the strips could be removed and used again on another shirt.

The blue wool cloth appears, from its undyed selvage edge, to be from the latter part of the nineteenth century. The metal conchos are manufactured from a contemporary material such as chrome, which does not have the warm luster of the German silver used on older shirts.

129

Numiipu (Nez Perce)
Cloak (back), about 1900
Collection history: Carl Schurz
collection, accessioned by NMAI in 1919
09.6567

In many contemporary Indian communities, ribbonwork shirts are a vibrant traditional link between the buffalo days and the present. Although today these garment materials are commercially manufactured and store-bought, the colors of the materials and the symbols incorporated into their designs have special meanings in the Plains Indian world. Interpretations vary, but there is general agreement about those meanings.

On the Fort Peck Indian Reservation in Montana in 1981, Patricia C. Bird, a Nakoda (Assiniboine-Sioux) cloth artist, designed and fabricated this contemporary appliqué ribbon shirt, made of yellow broadcloth, ribbons, and felt. As she explains:

> This contemporary men's ribbon shirt was designed for dress-up or for everyday wear. The designs are based upon the Sioux medicine wheel. The circular medicine wheel (with the crossed spokes) has many meanings, which vary from tribe to tribe. The round shape itself represents the circle of life and the disks remind us of blanket strip circles. The color for east is represented by yellow, the sacred plant for this direction is tobacco; south is represented by red (cedar); west is represented by black (sage); and north is represented by white (sweet grass). Turquoise-green symbolizes Mother Earth, and blue is the sky.

Feathers of the sacred golden eagle often adorn special items and clothing, and the cascading ribbons represent the flowing fringes of the war shirts.

131

Patricia C. Bird
Nakoda (Assiniboine–Sioux)
Ribbon Shirt (front), 1981
Fort Peck Indian Reservation, Montana

This shirt, with its rare combination of styles, signals the fading of the war-shirt tradition and the emergence of the ribbonwork style. The red wool, replacing animal-skin, represents an important material innovation, as wool was found to be more flexible than hide. Here the cross-grain use of the material allows the maker to use the selvage edge to create the bottom of the shirt. The sleeves were cut separately and attached to the body for efficient use of the cloth.

The Osage ribbonworker who made this shirt lived in or near Pawhuska, Oklahoma. She cut, folded, and overlaid exquisite multicolored silk ribbon strips on the wool, using her exceptional artistic skill to create complex patterns.

In the latter part of the nineteenth century, a delegation of Osage people traveled to Washington, D.C., to parley with United States government officials. While visiting the area, the Osage were invited to see U.S. marching troops and a military band. The Osage

were so impressed with the soldiers' and musicians' finery that government officials presented some of the uniforms and accoutrements to them. Upon returning home, a creative tribal member must have decided that these items could be worn only on special occasions, so the military coat, the hat with its high plume, and the epaulets became part of Osage women's wedding regalia.

Two contemporary Osage tribal members have determined that this shirt was made to be worn by a male and is an amalgam of many different styles. Traditional war shirts were poncho-like in construction; this shirt opens all the way down the front. The back of the shirt is more elaborately decorated than the front, with a neck piece, and locks of horsehair on the sleeves.

The red background color of this shirt contrasts with the black background of the Oto shirt 12.0838 (page 125), revealing the varied palette of color and vivid shifts afforded by using wool.

133

Wa-zha-zhe I-e (Osage)
Shirt (back), about 1900
Collection history: collected by Mark Raymond Harrington
near Pawhuska, Oklahoma, and accessioned by NMAI in 1908.
02.0663

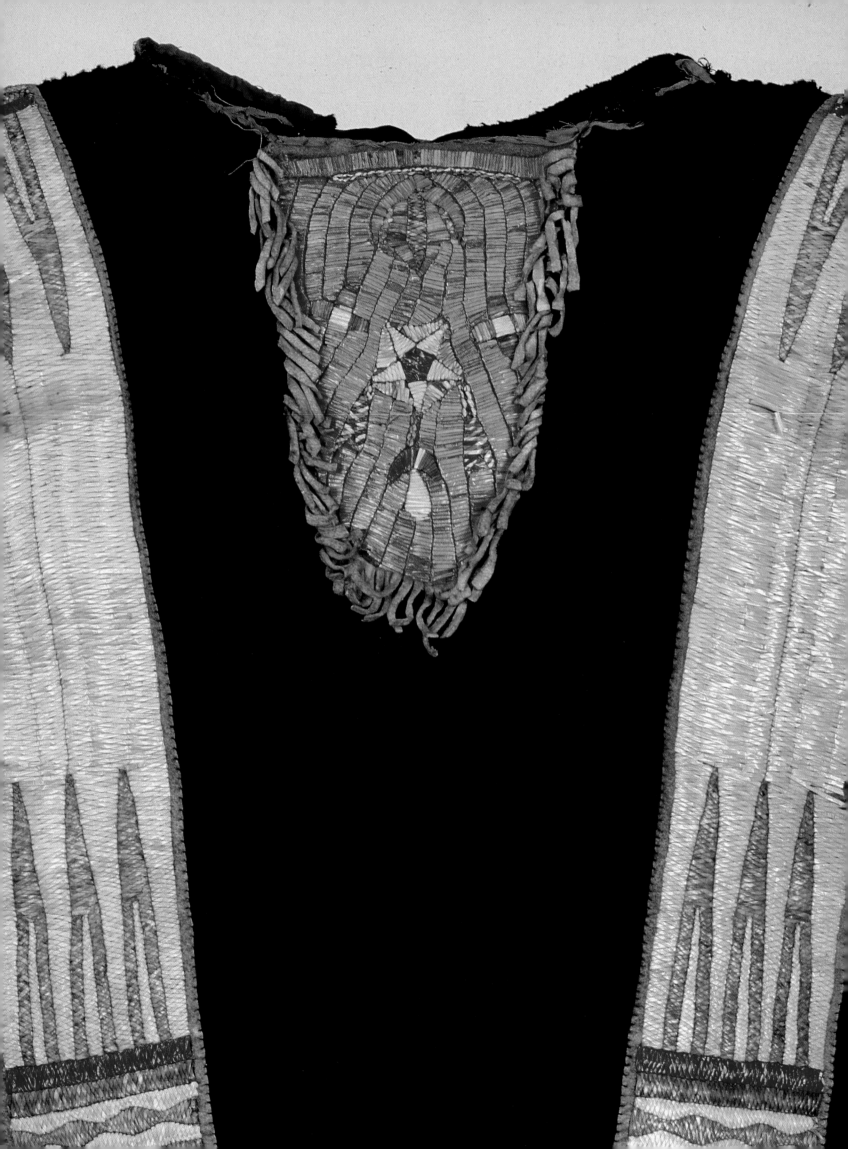

HUNDREDS OF YEARS AGO, life on the Plains was harsh, and artistic expression, like many other things, was minimal. The first decorative materials were probably paints; natural beads made of shells, bones, or other simple materials; and shapes cut out of natural materials. Probably the first sophisticated artform people developed on the Plains was porcupine quilling. When embroidered or wrapped on materials, quills are bright, colorful, and fragile. Because of quills' linear shape, many quillwork designs take on a box-like orientation, although some eastern Plains tribes created floral abstracts as well.

By the nineteenth century, large, glass pony beads had become available on the Plains, followed in the late 1840s by smaller seed beads. Beads changed the shape of the artistic landscape. They could take a linear orientation like quillwork, so existing tribal designs could still be used. But beads were easier to obtain than quills, and they offered a wider range of colors and the capacity to create more intricate designs. These new trade items generally—but not completely—replaced quills as an art medium.

With this growing mix of art media, some tribes began to specialize in creating a certain type of things. For example, the Lakota made many more baby carriers than the Blackfeet and A'aninin; the Crow created more gun cases than the Cheyenne; and the Lakota produced more tobacco bags than the Crow.

It is believed that the three tribes—Mandan, Hidatsa, and Arikara—who now reside on the Fort Berthold Indian Reservation in central North Dakota, and who have a long history of quillworking, continued to use that medium much longer than other tribes. They were so creative and prolific, it is believed these people made the majority of the quilled shirts that exist today. Early photographs reveal almost identical quilled shirts worn by the tribes of North Dakota; the A'aninin, Blackfeet, and Crow tribes of Montana; and others. The Crow undoubtedly maintained the quilling traditions of their sister tribe, the Hidatsa.

With the arrival of glass beads, quillwork steadily declined and almost faded from the world. The reintroduction of this distinctive Plains Indian tradition is due largely to the persistence and dedication of the Blue Legs and New Holy families of the Pine Ridge Indian Reservation in South Dakota. Quillwork can now be seen at most powwows in Indian country.

135

Plains Indian shirts are usually individual, one-of-a-kind expressions of aesthetic, mystical, and personal wonder. Sometimes, though, a style of shirt became so popular that it was copied, reproduced, and traded across the Plains and beyond. The similarity among these six shirts is remarkable—they are near duplicates of one another. All have a pullover construction; all but one are made of deerskin; all have leather fringes; all use yellow or orange quills worked in the multi-quill plait technique; and all use an elongated diamond or three-feather design motif. The resemblance among these shirts is not mere coincidence. Their tribal provenance as listed, is questionable. Museum accession records state that the shirts are: Arikara (14.1558), Mandan (24. 2563), Northern Blackfeet (22.7592), Atsina Gros Ventre (16.1235), Teton Sioux (12.2160), and Cheyenne (03.2624)—all different tribes of the northern Plains.

Determining their tribal origin and the reason or reasons for their wide distribution has challenged students of Plains Indian art. The multi-quill, plaited technique is an art style practiced by only a few interrelated tribes: the Crow of Montana; three tribes that now reside on the Fort Berthold Reservation in North Dakota—the Mandan, Arikara, and Hidatsa (who are closely related to the Crow)—and perhaps the Cree. At an earlier time it was believed that the Nez Perce people of Idaho also perfected this plaited style, but researchers may have determined that they probably obtained horsehair-wrapped quillwork and the plaited items associated with this style from their allies, the Crow. Although other tribes have displayed some familiarity with the process, the prolific experts at making plaited, quilled shirts appear to be limited to these groups.

The geographic distribution of these shirts could be explained in at least three ways: they may have been made as specialized trade items and dispersed through the North Dakota trade center, which ultimately reached all of the northern Plains tribes; they may have been presented as gifts to friends or visitors over a period of time; or they may have been copied by other tribes. Perhaps the truth lies in a combination of these possible explanations.

Richard Pohrt, Sr., a prominent Indian art expert of long standing, believes that the Mandan/Arikara/Hidatsa group, who live together, sustained quillworking traditions longer than the other tribes, making beautifully quilled items well into the 1930s. Their creations were distributed from the Red River to the north, to the Rocky Mountains. If this theory can be proved, we will know who made these beautiful shirts.

Pages 137–145: Various Plains Tribes
Quilled shirts, various dates
Collection history: various
14.1558, front

138

22.7592 back

143

16.1235 back

16.1235 back (detail)

"Some of our people will go and ask a person to take the shirt and be a keeper. Sometimes it's [inspired] by a dream. Maybe a person will dream about this war shirt and [being] the keeper of it. There is a pipe [that] goes with [the shirt]. The [old keeper] will always inform the new [keeper], how to use it. This is what you do with it. And today, just like the Medicine Pipe bundles, keepers have certain [restrictions]. No one will be able to sing the songs unless [they are] given the right to do that."
JOE OLD CHIEF (PIKUNI)

AS MENTIONED BEFORE, the first glass beads to reach much of the Plains were the pony beads, so called because they were carried in on the backs of the traders' ponies. These beads, which arrived in the early 1800s, and most subsequent ones were manufactured on the island of Murano, near Venice, Italy. Pony beads were colored only white, blue, black, and sometimes red, and the designs they produced were large and bulky.

Distinguishing tribal beadwork styles for the period before 1850 is difficult, if not impossible. The glass medium was new, and the women who were textile artists experimented with techniques and options. Small seed beads allowed beadwork patterns to become more refined and specific, and in a relatively short period of time certain tribal preferences began to take shape. For example, strong, solid patterns surrounded by free background space defined Lakota beadwork before the mid-1880s; later the patterns became more detailed, with spindly extensions filling previously open spaces.

Two basic methods of applying the beads evolved: the appliqué stitch, where the beads are sewn flat onto the item; and the lazy stitch, where the beads are strung and affixed to the item at regular intervals, forming a ribbed surface texture.

In a broad sense, prior to 1910, when the classic period ended, most Plains Indian tribes decorated many of their belongings with beads in some way. There were three important producers in the region: the Blackfeet, Crow, and Lakota. Each tribe's art style is different from the others'. The Blackfeet used the appliqué stitch, the Crow the modified lazy stitch, and the Lakota the lazy stitch. The three tribes' colors and patterns are distinct as well.

Like three stones dropped into a calm pond, these three styles of beadwork rippled outward from their centers of influence, becoming less distinct as they traveled. The smaller tribes who resided between these three cultural centers usually adapted a style derived from one of the original three.

147

Beadwork reached the height of its popularity around 1890. However, attractive beadwork is still produced by most Indian communities today.

This beaded shirt was produced in the classic Lakota style. Early shirts that featured quilled arm and chest strips were eventually replaced by shirts with beaded strips. The repeating beadwork pattern—bands of alternating color flanked by small triangular shapes—design, and use of color shown here are all characteristic of Lakota beadwork.

Similar to shirts numbered 12.0001 (page 37) and 01.3920 (page 45), this painted scalp shirt was worn by a person of great stature in traditional Lakota society. The Wicasas, or shirt wearers, were highly regarded for dedicating their lives to the welfare of their people. There are few examples of Wicasas' shirts still in existence. Most were painted like this shirt, the upper half blue, and the lower half yellow, symbolizing the sky and rock (Powell, 50).

The beadwork on this shirt was executed in the lazy stitch style. This technique allows the artist to cover large areas with beadwork, giving the appearance of beaded bands. Here, the artist took the opportunity to maximize the lazy stitch effects by incorporating small geometric patterns and alternate color schemes.

Lakota (Sioux)
Shirt (back), about 1875
Collection history: W. C. Whitty
collection, accessioned by NMAI in 1906.
00.9446

At first glance this shirt appears to be a fine example of a war shirt made in the north-western Plains area. The front of the shirt displays wide, strong strips and rosettes. The beadwork employs the appliqué technique, forming block-like patterns embellished with black-tipped, white, winter ermine skins. This type of finery is common on shirts made by the other tribes of the region, such as the Blackfeet groups, the A'aninin, and the Flathead. It was, however, collected from a reserve occupied by the Assiniboine.

The back of the shirt is unusual. A partial yoke of netted bugle beads is attached to the back of the shoulders in a style almost always worn by women. Even today, netted yokes are part of women's powwow attire, worn in one piece over a shawl or sewn to dancers' dresses to add color and beauty.

Cultural material in the Plains Indian world is filled with special innovations like this. These experiments may be original creations, or they may have been borrowed from other cultures. This dress yoke attached to a man's shirt may be such an experiment. The red yarn tufts highlighting the flowing ermine fur constitute another uncommon innovation.

The cut of the garment classifies it as being of relatively recent times. Older, classical shirts retain the leg skins as hanging pendants. As traditional materials became harder to find, styles changed. Shirts got shorter and shorter until today Plains shirts are similar in length to manufactured shirts.

151

Nakoda (Assiniboine)

Shirt (back), about 1885

Collection history: collected at Jack Pine, Alexis,

or Wabanum reserves (as noted in NMAI records), Alberta, Canada,

by Donald A. Cadzow, and accessioned by NMAI in 1926.

14.9264

Despite being made by different tribes separated by vast distances, many of the shirts in this exhibition employ similar materials, are constructed in similar ways, and reflect shared aesthetic and cultural values.

Most Plains Indian shirts have neck tabs or facings to reinforce that heavily used area. Their size and shape may differ, ranging from the triangles shown here, to rectangles, squares, U-shapes, or combinations of these. When there is no neck piece, a colorful cloth lining is often whipstitched around the opening. Despite these minor variations, the general cut of early garments and the placement of aesthetic accoutrements are remarkably similar among Plains Indian shirts.

Generally two decorative strips go over each shoulder and down the chest and back, covering the visible seams between the front leg skins, which form the sleeves, and the torso skins, which form the body. Here the beaded block/stripe motif on the strips has been applied with the modified lazy stitch, the preferred method of Crow artists. This technique provides a smooth texture to the beadwork. The red blocks in the shirt strip are made from tiny red beads, perhaps to resemble inserts of red wool, a common decoration in the early Crow shirts.

The curvilinear beaded patterns on the neck piece provide relief from the dominant geometric arrangements on this garment. Locks of dyed hair, not scalps, are attached to the outside of the chest and back strips, as well as on the back of the arm strips. This tells us that we are looking at the back of the shirt in this photograph. Otherwise, it can be difficult to distinguish the front of a Plains Indian shirt from the back, as they are often nearly identical.

153

Apsaalooke (Crow)
Shirt (back), about 1885
Collection history: purchase,
accessioned by NMAI in 1919.
09.1830

Plains Indian history is largely an oral tradition, rather than a written record. Therefore, we now know only a little about Plains life and culture during the early years, when the foundation for our art styles was formed. This shirt, for example, comprises several unusual elements, and it is impossible today to have a full understanding of its significance.

When viewed from the back, the shirt's feather design motifs and a floral neck piece could easily be identified as a beadwork interpretation of a North Dakota multi-plaited quillwork garment. The yellow beaded background and colorful patterns on the base of the feathers conform to this hypothesis.

The full opening in front is unusual for shirts of this type and could reflect a transitional influence. The long, colored fringes are typical of those created on the southern Plains.

It may be that the feather design of the north became so popular with some tribes that it was incorporated into different tribal styles and media.

Ponca

Shirt (front), about 1890

Opposite: back (detail)

Collection history: collected by Mark Raymond Harrington
in Oklahoma, and accessioned by NMAI in 1910.

03.6483

HISTORIC PHOTOGRAPHS

Photography courtesy of the National Museum of the American Indian, Smithsonian Institution;
all photographs ©Smithsonian Institution

Inside covers and above *Blackfeet men, Montana. Mary Roberts Rinehart collection, gift of Stanley Rinehart in 1961.*

Page 2 *Blackfeet men dressing for ceremonies.*

Page 16 *Blackfeet men, Montana. Mary Roberts Rinehart collection. Gift of Stanley Rinehart in 1961.*

Page 18 *Many Guns (Blackfeet), about 1903, Montana. Photo by Fred R. Meyer. David C. Vernon collection. Presented by Laurence S. Rockefeller.*

Page 20 *Spotted Rabbit (Absaroke [Crow]) on horseback, Montana. Photo by Fred E. Miller.*

Page 21 *Looking Glass (Nez Perce, 1823–77), on horseback, 1871, on the Yellowstone River near the mouth of the Shields River.*

Page 22 *Jingling Cloud and Two Stars (Wahpeton Sioux), about 1910, South Dakota. Photo by Alanson B. Skinner.*

Page 23 *Blackfeet man, Montana. Mary Roberts Rinehart collection, gift of Stanley Rinehart in 1961.*

Page 24 *Red Tomahawk (Blackfeet).*

(Note: familiar translations of tribal names arranged alphabetically; authentic tribal names are in parentheses)

BIBLIOGRAPHY

Ewers, John C. 1967. *The Blackfeet Raiders of the Northern Western Plains.* (Norman, Oklahoma: University of Oklahoma Press, 1967).

Ewers, John C. 1980. *Blackfeet Crafts.* (Stevens Point, Wisconsin: R. Schneider Publishers, 1980).

Gilman, Carolyn. 1987. *The Way to Independence: Memories of a Hidatsa Indian Family,* 1840–1920. (Saint Paul: Minnesota Historical Society Press, 1987).

Goetzmann, William H. 1984. Introduction to *Karl Bodmer's America.* (Omaha, Nebraska: Joslyn Art Museum and University of Nebraska Press, 1984).

Grinnell, George B. 1923. *The Cheyenne Indians: Their History and Way of Life.* (New Haven: Yale University Press, 1923).

Holm, Bill. 2000. Personal correspondence.

Keyser, James D. 1996. "Appointed Bison Robes: The Missing Link in the Biographic Art Style Lexicon," *Plains Anthropologist,* 41–155. (Lincoln, Nebraska: Journal of the Plains Anthropological Society, 1996).

Lester, Patrick D. 1995. *The Biographical Directory of Native American Painters.* (Norman, Oklahoma: University of Oklahoma Press, 1995).

Maurer, Evan M. 1992. *Visions of the People: A Pictorial History of Plains Indian Life.* (Minneapolis: The Minneapolis Institute of Arts, 1992).

Penney, David W. 1992. *Art of the American Frontier: The Chandler-Pohrt Collection.* (Seattle: University of Washington Press, 1992).

Pohrt, Richard. 2000. Personal correspondence.

Powell, Peter J. 1977. "Beauty for New Life: An Introduction to Cheyenne and Lakota Sacred Art," *The Native American Heritage: A Survey of North American Indian Art,* by Evan M. Maurer. (Chicago: Art Institute of Chicago, 1977).

Taylor, Colin F. 1984. "Analysis and Classification of the Plains Indian Ceremonial Shirt: John C. Ewers' Influence on a Plains Material Culture Project," *Fifth Annual Plains Indian Seminar in Honor of Dr. John C. Ewers.* (Cody, Wyoming: Buffalo Bill Historical Center, 1984).

Taylor, Colin F. 1984. "Crow Rendezvous," *Crow Indian Art.* (Valentine, Nebraska: L.T. Printing and Stationery, 1984).

Taylor, Colin F. 1993. *Saam.* (Germany: Verlag Für Amerikanistik/Wykauf Foehr, 1993).

Taylor, Colin F. 1998. *Buckskin & Buffalo: The Artistry of the Plains Indians.* (New York: Rizzoli International Publications, 1998).

Termin, Shawn. 2000. Personal correspondence.

Wissler, Clark. 1907. "Some Protective Designs of the Dakota," *Anthropological Papers of the American Museum of Natural History,* vol. I, Part II: 19–54, (1907).

Wissler, Clark. 1916. "Structural Basis to the Decoration of Costumes among the Plains Indians," *Anthropological Papers of the American Museum of Natural History,* vol. XVII, Part III, (1916).